THE GOOD COOK'S BOOK OF DAYS

a food lover's journal

Michele Anna Jordan

ILLUSTRATED BY MICHEL STONG

FROM THE
KITCHEN LIBRARY OF

ADDISON-WESLEY PUBLISHING COMPANY

Reading, Massachusetts   Menlo Park, California   New York
Don Mills, Ontario   Wokingham, England   Amsterdam   Bonn
Sydney   Singapore   Tokyo   Madrid   San Juan
Paris   Seoul   Milan   Mexico City   Taipei

FOR JAMES CARROLL,
my once and future editor

Copyright © 1995 by Michele Anna Jordan

ISBN 0-201-40659-4

Cover and interior illustrations by Michel Stong
Cover design by Suzanne Heiser
Text design by Karen Savary
Set in 12-point Bembo by Carol Woolverton Studio

1 2 3 4 5 6 7 8 9-DOC-98979695
First printing, September 1995

ALSO BY MICHELE ANNA JORDAN

A Cook's Tour of Sonoma

The Good Cook's Book of Oil & Vinegar

The Good Cook's Book of Mustard

The Good Cook's Book of Tomatoes

contents

The Good Cook's Archives

The Good Cook's Wine Cellar

acknowledgments

The Good Cook's Book of Days would not exist were it not for the efforts, cooperation, and talents of numerous people. More than any other single person, it is illustrator Michel Stong who has made this book beautiful, and I am honored to have my spare words in the company of her evocative drawings. Elizabeth Carduff, my editor at Addison-Wesley, worked extremely hard to make this project happen and I thank her profusely, as I do everyone at Addison-Wesley who assisted along the way: Beth Burleigh Fuller, Andrea Nelson, Jen Colton, and many others whose names I do not even know. Thanks, too, to my agent, Angela Miller, for her support of this book and for putting up with my occasionally unpredictable temperament. And, in an uncharacteristic burst of optimism, thanks in advance to the Addison-Wesley sales team for doing such a great job with this book.

I must also send a special *merci mille fois* to the utterly charming and gracious Jean-Jacques Vitrac, who in a most delicate, ethereal manner gave me Provence, its sky at sunset, its silvery olive trees, its liquid light, and so much more, when I most needed it. And *merci beaucoup aussi* to local Supervisor Ernie Carpenter, State Senator Mike Thompson, Select Sonoma County's executive director Betsy Timm, Michel Stong, Bill and Sandra MacIver of Matanzas Creek Winery, Gaye LeBaron of *The Press Democrat,* Daniel Patterson and Elizabeth Ramsey of Babette's Restaurant and Wine Bar, Ralph Tingle of Bistro Ralph, and the dozens of other people who encouraged and supported the formation of a formal sister relationship between Sonoma County and Provence, France.

Thanks also to Sara Peyton, my friend and co-worker at the *Sonoma County Independent,* for the warm review of *The Good Cook's Book of Tomatoes,* and for her friendship and support during the—what shall we call them, growing pains?—at the paper. And thanks, as well, to the elegant and articulate Flo Braker, author of such wonderful books as *The Simple Art of Perfect Baking,* for her generous, enthusiast support of *The Good Cook's* series and of my work in general.

My assistants Betty Ellsworth, Lesa Tanner, and Drea Moore deserve much more than a simple thank you, for they continue to help me make the crazy life of a writer possible and at least marginally manageable and sane. Liesel Hofman, my friend and copyeditor, goes to extraordinary lengths to be helpful and kind, often listening to and understanding my writer's woes more than anyone should have to: thank you, Liesel. Special thanks, as well, to Sandy Nelson for taking care of the feline trio, Mario, Marthilda, and Olive. Also to Tom Moore, Bob Didier, Marc Paisin, and Ana de Shore for taking good care of me. And to the thoroughly kind and wonderful Mary Duryee, an excellent cook herself, and her husband Guy Duryee, who have contributed more to my days and my nights than they will ever realize: *thank you,* again.

And now, on to my days and those who make them good, who share the difficulty when they're bad, and who, when inclination, geography, and time allow, celebrate them over wine, a good meal and, as often as possible, a great soundtrack: my beautiful daughters Gina and Nicolle; Ginny Stanford; Julieta Leil Weiss; Rob Cole; the Stong family: Michel, Jon, Griffin, and Jordan; Greil and Jenny Marcus; Jen Colton; Ridgely Evers and Colleen McGlynn; Madeleine Kamman; Jim Ford; Lou Preston; David Siracusa; Garrick Maul; Bob Sala; Nick Topolos; Egmont Tripp; Nancy Dobbs and John Kramer; Jerry and Patty Hertz; Elizabeth Ramsey and Daniel Patterson; and especially, John Boland and James Carroll.

introduction

It was just before Christmas, I think, when I went to the home of Michel Stong, the artist whose drawings enhance these pages, for dinner for the first time. Resting on a sideboard near the dining room table was a large open book of blank pages. Our menu had been written in Michel's fine hand; there was a place for each of us to sign our names, which we did. For the next couple of years, I watched the volume grow, a record of many wonderful afternoons, memorable evenings, special celebrations. I envied that book, the time for such attention to detail that it revealed, the moments of ephemeral pleasures that it captured, the occasional splatter of red wine upon a page. And so, when I am asked why I put together *The Good Cook's Book of Days,* that is the inspiration, the seed from which this little book grew.

I had long searched for a book like this, a beautiful place to record and preserve my day-to-day culinary life, but had failed to find it. How often I've been inspired by a few simple ingredients from the farm market or been struck by some delicious morsel I came across by accident, and how quickly I've forgotten the small details of the moment. Some of my finest gastronomic memories are of casual pleasures I have stumbled upon accidentally: a plum plucked from the tree as I walked down the hill to get the mail, a taco eaten at a roadside stand in Mexico at 7 A.M., bread and olive oil enjoyed in the golden light of an autumn afternoon, a quick meal prepared because old friends stopped by unexpectedly, a glass of wine I never want to forget. I wanted a place to record these details, other than the scribbled notes, random scraps of paper, and occasional printed menu that have served me until now. I will fill in the blanks in this book with great enthusiasm, and when one volume is full, I will start another, assuming that my life continues to be filled with good friends, memorable things to eat and drink, and, of course, the time to enjoy them. Today we are all so busy; this book betrays a wish, a plea, for time to savor the pleasures of life, so many of which emerge around a glass of wine and a loaf of good bread.

What I hope you will do with the *Book of Days* is use it as a diary and a journal, a menu planner, an organizer, a resource, but mostly as a source of inspiration. The pages designed for your insertions are meant to entice you, beckon you. The journal section is arranged by seasons, with a listing of the foods of each season, because it seems a sensible way not only to organize this record, but to reinforce that we are cyclical creatures, that we are defined by a natural ebb and flow of things. Many aspects of the modern world conspire to obscure the earth's rhythms; we are now farther removed from the seasons than we have ever been. The interplay of need and abundance, of longing and fulfillment, hunger and satiation, no longer controls our lives. Watermelons—from the southern hemisphere, of course—sit next to cranberries in the fall, apricots appear in the dead of winter, salmon is available year-round. Many find it difficult to recall what is in season, at its peak, when. This book is designed to help you remember.

Once I set out to put this book together, it took on a life of its own, growing into as much of a resource as into a culinary diary. Following the seasonal journal, *The Book of Days* is arranged to help you organize all aspects of your culinary life, from notes about memorable meals and the likes and dislikes of your friends and family, their birthdays and anniversaries, to the phone numbers and addresses of all your favorite stores and restaurants, as well as a couple of pages to record those of stores and mail-order sources that carry your favorite foods. In addition, there are charts and tables offering information on vinegars, oils, mustards, on storage requirements of common pantry items, and on equivalents, along with eight basic recipes to help you put together your own recipes and menus. The sources section lists nearly a hundred businesses and organizations that provide hard-to-find products and information on interesting and unusual culinary festivals; many culinary publications and organizations as well as cookbook stores are also noted.

The archives is a handy repository for details we all forget. Do you loan your cookbooks and then forget who has them? Keep a record of it here and it will be easy to retrieve—or at least to find—that favorite book. And what cook hasn't searched through stacks of books and magazines looking for a favorite recipe whose source has been forgotten? Here, you can record the location of nearly three hundred such recipes so that you can revisit them easily and efficiently. Finally, *The Good Cook's Book of Days* includes simple recipes, suggestions, tips, quotes, and anecdotes, all intended to assist you in being a good cook and a happy eater.

The Good Cook's
Journal of the Seasons

A recipe for Spring
Strawberries and Chèvre

First, you must find really good strawberries, small and sweet as they can be. Sprinkle the strawberries with a little granulated sugar and set them in a cool place for an hour or two.

Mix two cups of fromage blanc — fresh goat cheese — with a tablespoon or two of sugar, a teaspoon of pure vanilla extract, a teaspoon of grated fresh ginger, a tablespoon of finely minced candied ginger, a tablespoon of fresh lemon juice, and a teaspoon of grated lemon zest. Taste and add sugar until it is just right.

Sprinkle a tablespoon or two of your favorite balsamic vinegar over the strawberries and add a few turns of black pepper. Toss gently to combine the vinegar with the berries natural juices.

Spoon the cheese into the center of a beautiful platter and surround it with the strawberries. Eat it slowly, outside in the gentle spring sun, accompanied by the best champagne you can afford.

Asparagus

Arugula

Strawberries

Snow peas

Baby leeks

Spring lamb

Wild mustard greens

Morels

Boletus mushrooms

Bing cherries

Herring

Artichokes

New potatoes

Squash blossoms

Spinach

Spring salad greens

Goat cheeses

Better Boy &
Early Girl tomatoes

Texas 1015
Supersweet onions

Green garlic

Garlic fronds

Loquats

First corn

Vidalia onions

Fava beans

Asparagus

Arugula

Strawberries

Snow peas

Baby leeks

Spring lamb

Wild mustard greens

Morels

Boletus mushrooms

Bing cherries

Herring

Artichokes

New potatoes

Squash blossoms

Spinach

Spring salad greens

Goat cheeses

Better Boy &
Early Girl tomatoes

Texas 1015
Supersweet onions

Green garlic

Garlic fronds

Loquats

First corn

Vidalia onions

Fava beans

Asparagus

Arugula

Strawberries

Snow peas

Baby leeks

spring recipes

spring notes

March 19
American Chocolate Week

Asparagus is one of the first joys of spring, arriving about the same time as early strawberries. Instead of boiling or steaming asparagus, try roasting it. Roasted asparagus doesn't need to be peeled, and the process concentrates its delicate flavors. Simply snap off the tough end of each stalk of asparagus and place it in a heavy roasting pan. Drizzle about a tablespoon of pure olive oil over the asparagus, toss it so that it is evenly coated, and sprinkle with a little kosher salt and several turns of black pepper in a mill. Bake in a 500°F oven for 7 to 15 minutes, depending on the size of the stalks. Remove from the oven and serve with your favorite sauce.

To serve strawberries in their own juice, clean fresh spring berries and sprinkle them with a bit of granulated sugar. Refrigerate them for an hour or two before serving; the sugar will draw out their natural juices. To dress them up a bit, toss the strawberries with a tablespoon of balsamic vinegar and several turns of black pepper in a mill just before serving.

First Saturday in April
World Catfish Festival, Belzoni, Mississippi

Last Week in April
World's Biggest Fish Fry, Paris, Tennessee

To reduce the amount of oil in a salad dressing, use a milder vinegar (4 percent acidity, for example) and equal portions of oil and vinegar.

Today before a goblet of wine I was shamed,
My third cup unfinished, I couldn't pour another.
Wondering why I am always drunk beneath the flowers,
Perhaps the spring breeze has made me tipsy.
      —YÜAN CHEN, 9th Century

Salt improves the taste of almost everything, drawing the disparate elements of a dish together, unifying them, and, because it melts slowly on the tongue, contributing to the harmonious blending of flavors and creating a pleasing finish on the palate. Salt: it is flavor's midwife and no cook should be without it. There are several types, though the abundance common around the turn of the century no longer exists and most are hard to find. Sea salt has virtue to recommend it, though its form— superfine flakes or large, beautiful, impractical crystals—is less than ideal. Try the coarse flakes of kosher salt, the grains of which scatter across the tongue and melt like tiny stars, enchanting and mysterious, like taste itself.

Last Weekend in April
Vermont Maple Syrup Festival;
Asparagus Festival, Stockton, California

April
National Florida Tomato Month

To crave and to have are as like as a thing and its shadow. For when does a berry break upon the tongue as sweetly as when one longs to taste it, and when is the taste refracted into so many hues and savors of ripeness and earth, and when do our senses know a thing so utterly as when we lack it? And here again is a foreshadowing— the world will be made whole. For to wish for a hand on one's hair is all but to feel it. So whatever we may lose, very craving gives it back to us. Though we dream and hardly know it, longing, like an angel, fosters us, smoothes our hair, and brings us wild strawberries.

—MARILYNNE ROBINSON,
Housekeeping

May 8
National Herb Week

To preserve flavor, store olive oil in a cool, dark pantry, not in the refrigerator where its delicate flavors will be destroyed, nor next to the stove where heat will have the same effect.

Here's a little secret about spring. If you live close to a cultivated asparagus patch, take a look around a few weeks after it comes into season. Keep your eyes open for a slender green stalk, and if you find one, look for more. It will be the highly prized wild asparagus, an escapee from its cousin's more mannered environment. It is delicious: sweeter and more tender than the domesticated variety. Many aficionados prefer to eat wild asparagus raw to fully appreciate its delicacy.

Cherries are the first of summer's fruit, absolutely delicious in their own right, but also an intimation of what is soon to come. They have a painfully short season, which leads to a certain sense of urgency when they first appear. Better hurry, better eat as many as possible before they vanish. A fresh sweet cherry is irresistible; the rest of the year, use dried cherries, which are quite wonderful, especially with smoked poultry.

First weekend after Mother's Day
Vidalia Onion Festival, Vidalia, Georgia

As the winter snow melts and days grow warmer, the first of the year's mushrooms, the tantalizing morels, poke through the ground. Hunt for them in forests and meadows and near last year's forest fires, but do be sure you know exactly what you are looking for. If you have the slightest doubt, consult an expert. Morels fruit through early June. Add them to a soup or stew or enjoy them simply, sautéed in a little butter, seasoned with salt, pepper, and brandy, and finished with a little heavy cream.

The kitchen, reasonably enough, was the scene of my first gastronomic adventure. I was on all fours. I crawled into the vegetable bin, settled on a giant onion and ate it, skin and all. It must have marked me for life, for I have never ceased to love the hearty flavor of raw onions.

—JAMES BEARD, Delights and Prejudices

May 19–26
International Pickle Week

May 24
Anti-Saloon League founded, 1893

Grilled green onions are common at road-side taco stands throughout Mexico, and easy to duplicate at home. Simply rub a bunch of cleaned scallions (about 12) with a bit of olive oil and roast them in a 375°F oven or grill them on a stove-top grill until they are limp and tender. Serve them wrapped in a warm corn tortilla or with steamed rice and plenty of your favorite salsa. You can prepare baby leeks in the same way.

To make a simple yet versatile and delicious mustard cream, mix together 1¼ cups crème fraîche (or 1 cup sour cream thinned with ¼ cup half-and-half) with ¼ cup Dijon mustard, 1 teaspoon kosher salt, and 1 teaspoon freshly ground pepper. You can use it immediately or refrigerate it up to 10 days. Serve as a dip with vegetables or prawns; as a topping for split pea soup; as a dressing for potato salad, grated celery root, or avocados filled with smoked chicken and fennel; or alongside grilled or broiled fish, carpaccio, paté, or roast beef.

The discovery of a new dish does more for human happiness than the discovery of a new star.
—JEAN ANTHELME BRILLAT-SAVARIN, The Physiology of Taste

*Third weekend in May
World Championship Barbecue
Cooking Contest,
Memphis, Tennessee*

Bats, perhaps the most misunderstood animals on the planet, are essential pollinators of a huge variety of plants, including many delicious foods both in the United States and throughout the world; over 450 cash crops—mangos, guavas, dates, figs, and avocados, for example—rely upon bats' natural activity to reproduce and, sometimes, to survive. As the only nocturnal predators of insects, bats perform a fundamental task as they go about their nightly meal, reducing not only populations of mosquitoes, but other harmful pests that left unchecked would decimate numerous important crops. Bats, whose nearly one thousand types make up 25 percent of all the earth's mammals, are among the longest-lived (up to thirty years) animals for their size, are not related to rodents, and are extremely intelligent. Without bats, the ecological balance of the planet would be shattered.

A recipe for Summer Aioli

To make aioli, peel a handful of fresh garlic,
preferably from a friend who's grown it.
Place the cloves in a large stone mortar
and add a teaspoon of coarse salt.

Have two cups of olive oil (Provençal, Tuscan, or Ligurian)
nearby.

Using a wooden or stone pestle, pound the garlic into a
liquidy pulp. Add a deeply colored egg yolk from a
chicken allowed to run free, and then add another
egg yolk, gently mixing with the pestle.

Begin to pour a thin trickle of olive oil into the side of the
mortar, beating with the pestle all the while. Continue
until all the oil has been incorporated.
Smear the aioli on toasted slices of baguettes and spoon
flavorful bouillabaisse broth over them. Though not
traditional (for that you must make rouille), this is
very, very good. Pass the platters piled high with
the fish, mussels, and crabs of the bouillabaisse.

If you can, do this in the south of France near the sea,
where the sky is the color of periwinkles and the light
liquid and buttery.

Apricots

Peaches

Nectarines

Garlic

Raspberries

Blueberries

Blackberries

Watermelons

Cantaloupes

Honeydew melons

Sharlyn melons

Charentais melons

Crenshaw melons

Crane melons

Queen Anne cherries

Wild salmon

Tomatoes

Nasturtiums

Fresh herb flowers

Sweet basil

Cilantro

Zucchini

Soft-shell crab

Peppers of all types

Corn

Avocados

Lavender

Papayas

Mangos

Okra

Grape leaves

Walla Walla onions

Baby torpedo onions

Lemon cucumbers

Santa Rosa plums

Gravenstein apples

Haricots verts

Apricots

_____	Peaches	_____
_____	Nectarines	_____
_____	Garlic	_____
_____	Raspberries	_____
_____	Blueberries	_____
_____	Blackberries	_____
_____	Watermelons	_____
_____	Cantaloupes	_____
_____	Honeydew melons	_____
_____	Sharlyn melons	_____
_____	Charentais melons	_____
_____	Crenshaw melons	_____
_____	Crane melons	_____
_____	Queen Anne cherries	_____
_____	Wild salmon	_____
_____	Tomatoes	_____
_____	Nasturtiums	_____
_____	Fresh herb flowers	_____
_____	Sweet basil	_____

June
National Dairy Month

Basil—its fresh, evocative scent, its compelling flavor—has become synonymous with summer. Don't let the season pass without stocking up on pesto. To preserve it through the fall, simply purée basil leaves with olive oil (about $^3/_4$ to 1 cup extra-virgin olive oil to 4 cups of fresh basil leaves). Pack it in portions you will use in one recipe and float a bit of olive oil over the surface. Freeze the purée until you are ready to use it. To complete your pesto, add 4 to 5 cloves of garlic, $^1/_4$ cup pine nuts, and 1 teaspoon kosher salt to each cup of basil purée. Mix well in a food processor, transfer to a mixing bowl, and blend in 3 tablespoons softened butter and 3 tablespoons freshly grated Parmigiano cheese.

 The best way to peel a tomato is to place it—through its blossom end— on the tines of a fork and scorch the skin over a gas flame. Turn the fork quickly so that the flesh doesn't begin to cook; it will take 5 to 15 seconds per tomato, depending on size. A boiling-water bath does loosen the skins, but it also dilutes the tomato's flavor.

July 3
M. F. K. Fisher born, 1908

July 14
Bastille Day;
Chez Panisse Garlic Festival,
Berkeley, California

Slice ripe peaches or nectarines, sprinkle a little sugar over them, followed by a squeeze of lemon juice and a splash of muscat wine. Serve chilled.

Never refrigerate a raw tomato. Store at temperatures above 55°F and use within 3 to 4 days. To save tomatoes about to turn, chop them and cover them with vinegar or olive oil. Then store in the refrigerator and use within a day in a sauce, salsa, or vinaigrette.

Apricots come into full season quickly and do not linger for long. If you don't pay attention, you can miss them entirely. To capture their enticing flavor, make apricot chutney. In a large, heavy pot combine 5 pounds apricots (halved and stones removed) with 3 pounds sugar, 1 pound currants, $1/2$ cup minced fresh garlic, 5 jalapeño peppers (stemmed and cut into thin julienne), 5 ounces fresh minced ginger, $1/2$ ounce dried hot chilies, 3 cups apple cider vinegar, and 2 tablespoons kosher salt. Stir until the sugar has dissolved and then simmer over low heat for about an hour. Ladle into sterilized pint or half-pint jars and process in a water bath for 15 minutes. You can make a similar chutney with summer peaches.

Second week in July
National Cherry Festival, Traverse City,
Michigan, the "Cherry Capital of the World"

Third weekend in July
Pork, Peanut, and Pine Festival,
Surry, Virginia

For delightful (and healthy) summer desserts, grill fruit over the cooling coals after a barbecue. Fresh apricot halves take about 3 minutes on each side; serve them with a squeeze of lime juice and a little brown sugar. Peaches, cut in half, take slightly longer until they are heated through and just tender. After removing them from the grill, spoon into their centers fresh goat cheese (fromage blanc) that you have mixed with a bit of vanilla, sugar, grated fresh ginger, candied ginger, and lemon juice.

Last weekend in July
Gilroy Garlic Festival,
Gilroy, California

When one has tasted watermelons, one knows what angels eat. It was not a Southern watermelon that Eve took; we know it because she repented.

—MARK TWAIN

In the south of France, garlic harvest is celebrated as Aioli Monstre, *a feast during which the freshest vegetables, salt cod, bread, and plenty of red wine are served with aioli, a robust garlic mayonnaise. It's an easy meal to create yourself. Place 15 cloves of fresh garlic in a large marble mortar, add 2 to 3 teaspoons kosher salt, and pound with a wooden pestle until the garlic is reduced to a nearly liquid paste. Add 2 egg yolks and, using the pestle, incorporate them into the garlic. Pour in your best extra-virgin olive oil—about 1^1/$_2$ cups in all—in a very thin stream and beat continuously with the pestle. As the mixture thickens, increase the flow of the olive oil slightly. Taste the sauce, add the juice of ^{1}/$_2$ lemon and, if necessary, thin with 1 or 2 teaspoons of warm water. Refrigerate the aioli, covered, until ready to serve.*

In June, the first of summer's corn coincides with the last of the year's cherries. Capture the moment in a cherry & corn salsa, delightful with gravlax or fresh grilled salmon. Toss 1 pound Bing cherries, cut in half and pitted, with about a cup and a half of very fresh corn kernels, quickly cooked and then cut from the cob. Add 2 chopped shallots, 1 chopped jalapeño pepper, 2 teaspoons finely chopped mint, a teaspoon fresh thyme leaves, 3 tablespoons unrefined corn oil (or olive oil), 2 tablespoons medium-acid vinegar (cherry, raspberry, or sherry), and $1/2$ teaspoon kosher salt. Let rest for 30 minutes before serving.

July
National Blueberries Month;
Jasmine flowers in full bloom

Should you be lucky enough to find yourself with an abundance of summer berries— raspberries, blackberries, blueberries—preserve their essence in homemade fruit vinegar. Add twice as much fruit as white wine vinegar to a glass jar or crock, cover, and store in a cool cupboard or refrigerator for 2 to 10 days, tasting regularly to determine when your berry vinegar is sufficiently flavored. Strain it through cheesecloth or a paper coffee filter, bottle your vinegar, and store in a cool, dark cupboard. You can make peach, nectarine, or apricot vinegar by the same method.

Take advantage of the sun's free energy to make sun tea. Just fill a glass jar or pitcher with water, add the tea, and place it in the sun for an hour or two, until the tea is as weak or strong as you prefer. Chill and serve over ice.

First weekend in August
International Pinot Noir Festival,
McMinnville, Oregon

August 5
National Mustard Day

Ripe, tangy tomatoes: summer's pride. Enjoy them now, and let them be just a memory during the months when they taste like little more than soggy cardboard. For a simple dish, peel 4 medium tomatoes and cut them into wedges. Heat a little olive oil in a sauté pan and cook the tomatoes quickly, about 2 minutes on each side. Season with a squeeze of lemon, salt, and black pepper; scatter minced scallions over them or top them with some finely minced garlic and very thin strips of basil. Serve immediately as a side dish, with some chèvre and good bread alongside.

August 8
Sneak Some Zucchini onto Your
Neighbors' Porch Night

For a refreshing late-summer snack, place a bunch or two of grapes (organic, please!) in the freezer until they are frozen solid. They are great on swelteringly hot days, and kids love them.

August 15
Julia Child born, 1912

August 17
Watermelon Festival,
Hope, Arkansas

One of the simplest pleasures of summer is a salad of sliced tomatoes, variations of which are nearly endless. To serve 4, slice 4 large tomatoes through their equators—horizontally, not vertically—arrange them on 1 large or 4 small plates, drizzle with extra-virgin olive oil, and sprinkle with a little kosher salt and freshly ground pepper. Dress up the salad with minced Italian parsley and garlic, grated Parmigiano cheese, fresh basil and slices of mozzarella fresca, thin slices of Meyer lemon, anchovy fillets, sliced olives, or tinned sardines and thin slices of onion.

August
Aioli Monstre *celebrated in Provence*

A recipe for fall

eat daily from August
until the first
winter storm

A loaf of good, hearty bread
tomatoes fresh from the garden
and warm from the sun

the best extra virgin
olive oil you
can find

salt and pepper

a glass of red wine

tear off a chunk of bread and place
in a hot oven. Slice the tomatoes into
thick rounds and lay them on a plate.
Drizzle with a little olive oil and a
sprinkling of salt and pepper. Get the
bread from the oven, pour olive oil all
over it and then some salt and
pepper. Take your bread, tomatoes,
and glass of wine outside or to the
nearest westward window. Watch
the light change.

Boletus mushrooms

Hen-of-the-Woods
mushrooms

Beets

Fennel

Cranberries

Pomegranates

Chanterelles

Eggplant

Olives

New olive oil

Artichokes

Winter squashes

Figs

White truffles

Grapes

Spinach

Sorrel

Fall salad greens

Radicchio

_____ Walnuts _____

_____ Boletus mushrooms _____

_____ Hen-of-the-Woods _____
mushrooms

_____ Beets _____

_____ Fennel _____

_____ Cranberries _____

_____ Pomegranates _____

_____ Chanterelles _____

_____ Eggplant _____

_____ Olives _____

_____ New olive oil _____

_____ Artichokes _____

_____ Winter squashes _____

_____ Figs _____

_____ White truffles _____

_____ Grapes _____

_____ Spinach _____

_____ Sorrel _____

_____ Fall salad greens _____

Radicchio

Walnuts

Boletus mushrooms

Hen-of-the-Woods
mushrooms

Beets

Fennel

Cranberries

Pomegranates

Chanterelles

Eggplant

Olives

New olive oil

Artichokes

Winter squashes

Figs

White truffles

Grapes

Spinach

Sorrel

fall notes

September
Cranberry Festival, Bandon, Oregon;
National Organic Harvest Month

Weekend following Labor Day
Castroville Artichoke Festival,
Castroville, California

Beets are available year-round but are at their natural peak in late summer and early fall. In addition to the familiar red beet, there are several other varieties, all absolutely delicious. Look for golden beets, white beets, and the red and white striped beets called Chioggia. Rather than boiling them, concentrate their flavors by roasting them whole in the oven. Rub trimmed, unpeeled beets with a little olive oil, place them on a baking rack in a 350°F oven and roast until tender, from 45 to 90 minutes, depending on size. Remove them from the oven and allow to cool before peeling them. Serve them cut in quarters and tossed with toasted walnuts, crumbled Roquefort cheese, a splash of olive oil, and plenty of fresh ground pepper.

To preserve a piece of fresh ginger, place it whole or sliced in a jar and cover it with rice wine vinegar. Slice off or remove pieces as you need them. Use the vinegar, too, which will be evocatively perfumed with the aroma of ginger. Stored in a cool, dark cupboard, both the ginger and the vinegar should keep for about a year.

Mini-pumpkins make colorful decorations, but they are also delicious to eat. Bake them in a 350°F oven until they are tender, about 40 minutes (or punch a few holes in them and cook in the microwave for about 10 minutes), cut off the stem ends, scoop out the seeds, and fill with your favorite risotto or several cloves of roasted garlic.

September 26
Johnny Appleseed born, 1774

To dry chilies at home, thread them through their stems on string and hang them several feet above a wood stove until they are dried. Store them in the pantry or the kitchen and remove them as needed.

Second weekend in October
Gumbo Festival, Bridge City, Louisiana

The olive tree is surely the richest gift of Heaven.
—THOMAS JEFFERSON, Letter to George Wythe

Although figs come into season in midsummer, by fall there is an urgent abundance. A fresh fig has a brief life and moves quickly from its soft and yielding appeal to collapse and decay. Keep figs for only a day or two in the refrigerator. To make a simple fig chutney, purée 10 ripe figs with 3 cloves garlic, 1 to 2 tablespoons lemon juice, 1 teaspoon kosher salt, 2 teaspoons toasted and crushed cumin seed, ¹/₂ teaspoon red pepper flakes, and 1 cup water. 75 Store in the refrigerator and serve as a condiment with yogurt, curry, or roasted meats and poultry.

October 8–15
American Beer Week

September–October
Oktoberfest celebrations held all over the world

In Latin America, Día de los Muertos—*Day of the Dead, from which our Halloween has evolved—is celebrated on November 1 and 2. Graves and entire cemeteries are decorated, and altars are built to honor departed loved ones, who, according to tradition, return to partake of the sensual pleasures of the flesh that are denied them in the spirit world. Loved ones' favorite dishes along with traditional foods like* panes de muertos, *a sweet, dark bread flavored with anise and baked in human and animal shapes, are added to the altars. In a particularly touching gesture, many Mexican families hang baskets of traditional foods outside their homes so that passing spirits without families or friends will have something to eat.*

When you purchase vinegar, be sure to check the level of acidity, expressed either as a percentage as in, say, 6 percent, or in grain, as in 60 grain. The higher the number, the greater the amount of acetic acid and the stronger the vinegar will be.

October
International Association of Culinary Professionals' Cookbook Month;
Pumpkin festivals held throughout the country

Medieval people ate between 10 and 20 grams of salt a day, far more than the average modern American. . . . On the table, salt was kept in salt cellars, elaborate contraptions of precious metals, often sculpted into shells, dragons, or ships as high as two feet. They became most important utensils, embodying not only expense and artistry, but the potency of salt's supposed magic, its ability to spread evil if mishandled, bring luck if treated with care. Cellars were symbols of wealth, status, and superstition. The salt itself was carefully piled in the center—perhaps in the hold of a perfect ship with eight miniature crewmen—and rounded into a small white mountain.

—SALLIE TISDALE, Lot's Wife

Fresh fennel has a delightfully delicate, fragrant flavor. It is outstanding cut in half, browned, and then braised until tender in olive oil and white wine. It is equally delicious shaved very thinly, tossed with extra-virgin olive oil and fresh lemon juice, and served with thin curls of Parmigiano cheese scattered over the surface.

Last Sunday in October
Saffron Rose Festival, Consuegra, Spain

October–December
The first of the year's olives are harvested in California and in Europe, and the new olive oil is pressed

Tapenade, a paste of puréed olives, anchovies, garlic, and various other ingredients, is a versatile and enticing condiment. It can be combined with a good mayonnaise for a sandwich spread or thinned with olive oil and a bit of warm water for a simple pasta sauce. It is excellent as a garnish with baked goat cheese and delicious served just with hot bread. To make a simple tapenade, purée together 1/2 cup pitted Kalamata olives, 2 or 3 cloves garlic (peeled), 2 or 3 anchovy fillets, 1 tablespoon Dijon mustard, 1 tablespoon minced fresh Italian parsley, and 1/2 cup extra-virgin olive oil. Store in the refrigerator for up to 10 days.

October 31
All Hallows' Eve

 Pomegranates are the first, and arguably the most beautiful, of fall fruits. They also disappear quickly. You can stretch their season through the holidays by buying several at the peak of the season and then seeding them. Fill pint jars or plastic bags with the ripe seeds and freeze them. They make a beautiful and delicious addition to rice salads and are lovely scattered over sliced oranges.

November 1
All Saints' Day

Most commercial flavored oils are, in spite of their current popularity, a waste of money (sad but true); even those made at home are of limited value. If you must, make them with room-temperature, good-quality olive oil, blanch and dry fresh herbs before using them, and make the oil in small quantities that will be used within a day or two. Homemade flavored oils must be refrigerated.

Regardless of when you purchase them, most mature potatoes are harvested from September through November. Potatoes keep well, provided they are stored properly, between 45° and 50°F and away from light. Onions prefer these conditions, too. But never store the two vegetables together; each gives off a gas that shortens the life of the other.

Cranberries are harvested in the fall and begin appearing in the marketplace in late September and early October. Cranberry vinegar makes a dazzling holiday gift and is very easy to prepare. Chop cranberries in a food processor and for each 4 cups of berries, add 2 cups of white wine vinegar. Let the mixture sit in a glass jar or crock, covered, in a cool pantry or refrigerator for about a week. Strain through several layers of cheesecloth or a paper coffee filter. Pour the cranberry vinegar, which will be the color of liquid rubies, into slender bottles of clear glass. Add a long thin twist of orange zest or several fresh cranberries threaded on a wooded skewer to each bottle and close with a cork. Store in a cool dark cupboard until ready to use.

November 12–19
National Culinary Week

November 15
National Clean Out Your Refrigerator Day

Third Thursday in November
The fall's new vintage of Beaujolais
Nouveau is released in France

Sweet potatoes, native to America and members of the morning glory family, are delicious baked in the oven, sliced in lengthwise wedges, baked again, and then drizzled with a bit of your favorite vinaigrette. They are also packed with good-for-you substances, including vitamin A (more than almost any other food) and antioxidants, which are said to slow the aging process and prevent cancer.

A recipe for Winter
Tomato and Bread Soup

On a cold winter night when you need the quick comfort of good soup, try this one — a traditional Italian bread soup full of simple good flavors. For four people, sauté a handful of peeled and chopped garlic in olive oil.

Add four cups of diced tomatoes — those that you canned a few months earlier are ideal — and simmer for five minutes.

Add four cups of chicken stock, return to a simmer, add several turns of black pepper and coarse salt to taste.

Have three cups of bread cubes — torn from crusty, coarse grain, day-old bread into uneven pieces — divided among four bowls. Ladle the soup over the bread and let it sit for five minutes so that the bread soaks up some of the juices. Just before serving, drizzle a tablespoon or two of extra-virgin olive oil over the soup and scatter a tablespoon of chopped Italian parsley and a few turns of black pepper over the top.

Eat this by a roaring fire, with good friends gathered around you and a cat asleep on the hearth.

Brussels sprouts

Broccoli rabe

Oysters

Crab

Clams

Blood oranges

Broccoli

Kiwifruit

Rutabagas

Turnips

Persimmons

Black truffles

Winter salad greens

Pears

Celery root

Quince

Grapefruit

Meyer lemons

Oranges

Mussels

Brussels sprouts

Broccoli rabe

Oysters

Crab

Clams

Blood oranges

Broccoli

Kiwifruit

Rutabagas

Turnips

Persimmons

Black truffles

Winter salad greens

Pears

Celery root

Quince

Grapefruit

Meyer lemons

Oranges

Mussels

Brussels sprouts

Broccoli rabe

Oysters

Crab

Clams

Blood oranges

Broccoli

Kiwifruit

Rutabagas

Turnips

Persimmons

Black truffles

Winter salad greens

Pears

Celery root

Quince

Grapefruit

November 22
French chef and author
Madeleine Kamman's birthday

To make crème fraîche, a fresh cultured cream common in Europe that resembles a sort of suave sour cream, scald a pint glass jar and its lid with boiling water. Dry it thoroughly, add 1 or 2 cups heavy cream and 2 or 3 tablespoons cultured buttermilk. Close the jar and shake it for about 30 seconds to mix it well. Set it in a warm place—about 70°F is ideal—for around 24 hours, until it is thick. Stir well and refrigerate. The crème fraîche will keep for at least 10 days.

HOW TO CURE A COLD:  *one tall silk hat, one four-poster bed, one bottle of brandy. To be taken as follows: put the tall silk hat on the right-hand post at the foot of the bed, lie down and arrange yourself comfortably, drink the brandy, and when you see a tall silk hat on both the right and* left *bedposts you are cured.*

—An old French proverb, *in* **M. F. K. FISHER**, A Cordiall Water

Rosemary is a hearty—and deliciously fragrant—herb that grows easily and abundantly. If you live in a warm climate without harsh winters, plant it directly in the ground. Otherwise, plant your rosemary in a pot that you can bring inside for the winter. When you need a little for a recipe, simply snip off a sprig.

December 5
Prohibition ended, 1933

December 22
California Kiwifruit Day

Nothing is so effective in keeping one young and full of lust as a discriminating palate thoroughly satisfied at least once a day.

—*Angelo Pelligrini,*
The Unprejudiced Palate

For a delicious winter salad, peel and slice several oranges (blood oranges, if you can find them) and arrange them on a plate. Drizzle with the best Italian olive oil you can find and then add a bit of kosher salt and several turns of black pepper in a mill. Use a vegetable peeler to shave off thin strips of Parmigiano or Romano cheese and scatter the strips over the oranges. Serve with winter greens alongside and a light-bodied red wine.

Potato soup is a delicious winter staple. If you can make it on top of a wood-burning stove, so much the better, but any source of heat, even a hot plate in a tiny apartment, will do. Just sauté a couple of yellow onions in some olive oil until they are very soft. Add 4 or 5 russet potatoes (about 3 pounds, scrubbed and diced) and cover it all with 8 cups stock, water, or a combination of both. Simmer until the potatoes are tender, about 20 minutes. Purée with an immersion blender, season with salt and pepper, and add whatever else you like: 3 cups grated Cheddar cheese, chopped fresh spinach sautéed in olive oil and garlic, sautéed garlic and a can of diced tomatoes, a puréed chipotle pepper and spicy sausages, 3 cups cooked broccoli.

December
Congress adopts the Volstead Act to enforce the Eighteenth Amendment, prohibiting the manufacture, sale, transportation, import, or export of alcoholic beverages, 1919

January 6
*Feast of the Epiphany, oldest Christian holiday
(also celebrated as Twelfth Night, Three Kings
Day, Feast of Jordan, and Old Christmas Day)*

A pear poached in red wine is a simple yet exquisite treat. Begin with a peeled pear for each serving, cut it in half, and remove the core. Place the pears in a heavy pot that just holds them in a single layer. Open a bottle of light- or medium-bodied red wine, pour yourself a glass, and then pour the rest over the pears. Add enough water to just cover them. Simmer over medium heat until the pears are tender and then transfer them with a slotted spoon to a serving platter. Keep the pears warm or chill them. Add $1/2$ cup sugar to the poaching liquid, turn the heat to high, and reduce the liquid until it is thick and syrupy. Drizzle the syrup over the pears and serve them immediately, accompanied by a glass of red wine.

January 21
International Hot and Spicy Food Day

To avoid the refined and artificially saturated fats used in margarine, make a blend of equal parts of butter and extra-virgin olive oil. Bring the butter to room temperature and stir in the oil until the mixture is smooth. Store, covered, in the refrigerator until ready to use.

Thinness is a horrible calamity for women: beauty to them is more than life itself, and it consists above all of the roundness of their forms and the graceful curvings of their outlines. The most artful toilette, the most inspired dressmaker, cannot disguise certain lacks, nor hide certain angles; and it is a common saying that a scrawny woman, no matter how pretty she may look, loses something of her charm . . . for women who are born thin and whose digestion is good, we cannot see why they should be any more difficult to fatten than young hens; and if it takes a little more time than with poultry, it is because human female stomachs are comparatively smaller, and cannot be submitted, as are those devoted barnyard creatures, to the same rigorous and punctually followed diet.

—JEAN ANTHELME BRILLAT-SAVARIN, The Physiology of Taste

Brussels sprouts, high in vitamins A and C as well as several substances believed to fight infections and inhibit cancers, are one of our most maligned vegetables. But cooked properly (rather than nearly to mush, the reason for their poor reputation), they are a delight. Simmer Brussels sprouts briefly—5 to 10 minutes, depending on their size—and drain them. Serve with a drizzle of lemon juice and a spicy aioli.

January 23
National Pie Day

BUTTER: *Butter may be made from any kind of milk, but the fattest and richest is made from ewe's milk. In every country where I have traveled I have never failed to obtain fresh-churned butter. Wherever I went, I procured cow's, camel's, mare's, or ewe's milk. I filled a bottle with it three quarters full, stoppered it, and fastened it to my horse's neck. My horse did the rest. When I arrived at my destination, I unstoppered the bottle, and there was a piece of butter as large as my fist.*

—Alexander Dumas's
Dictionary of Cuisine

In the late winter in the Northeast, when the days have grown warm but the nights are still freezing, the sap of the maple tree begins to flow. With snow still on the ground, you can find buckets attached to the trees, collecting the precious liquid that will be boiled down to produce the famous authentic maple syrup, of which there is nowhere near as much as we wish.

February
National Cherry Month

For a change from the ubiquitous cranberry-orange relish, make cranberry soup as part of a festive holiday meal. Simmer a package of cranberries, 3 whole cloves, and a piece of cinnamon with a cup of orange juice, a cup of red wine, a cup of water, and $2/3$ cup sugar until the cranberries are soft. Purée and strain or press the mixture through a food mill. Serve hot or chilled, garnished with orange zest and a dollop of crème fraîche.

For a simple, satisfying meal when you are tired from, say, holiday shopping, try this easy recipe. Cook 2 or 3 ounces dried spaghetti for each portion. Drain the spaghetti thoroughly, place it in a large bowl, and toss it with enough full-flavored extra-virgin olive oil to coat it thoroughly. Add $1/4$ teaspoon ground nutmeg, $3/4$ teaspoon freshly ground black pepper, and $1/4$ teaspoon kosher salt per portion, and toss again. Serve immediately with hot bread, a big green salad, and a glass of light-bodied red wine.

Whenever you find yourself with an abundance of fresh lemons, preserve them. To make a quart, slice about a dozen small lemons lengthwise into sixths. Toss them with ³/4 cup kosher salt and 1 tablespoon sugar, and pack them into a clean quart jar. Add 1 cup fresh lemon juice, cover the jar, and place it in a cool cupboard for 7 days, turning it upside down each morning and righting it at night, so that all the lemons spend time in the liquid. On the seventh day, top off the jar with olive oil. If you will use the lemon slices within a month or so, there is no need to refrigerate them, for that would blunt their flavor. Use preserved lemons as a garnish, or in salads, soups, curries, and rice dishes, or as a simple, tangy snack.

To feel safe and warm on a cold wet night, all you really need is soup.
—Laurie Colwin,
Home Cooking

February 11
Cookbook Festival, Fargo, North Dakota

Polenta is an ideal comfort food, perfect for any meal during the dark days of December and January. By far the easiest way to make it is to place 1 cup coarse-ground polenta into a 2-quart baking dish, add 4 cups water, 2 teaspoons kosher salt, 2 tablespoons butter cut in pieces, and stir. Place it in a 325°F oven for 40 minutes. Open the oven, give the polenta a quick stir, and cook it for an additional 10 minutes. Serve immediately with your favorite topping or sauce: maple syrup for breakfast, Gorgonzola cheese and toasted walnuts for breakfast or dinner, Parmigiano cheese and fresh sage for any meal, simple marinara sauce at any time. The possibilities are limited only by your preferences.

*Last week of February
American Wine Appreciation Week*

The Good Cook's

Resources

restaurants

I never eat in a restaurant that's over a hundred feet off the ground and won't stand still.

—CALVIN TRILLING

NAME _____ PHONE _____
ADDRESS _____
HOURS _____ PRICE _____
FAVORITE DISHES _____
_____
_____

NAME _____ PHONE _____
ADDRESS _____
HOURS _____ PRICE _____
FAVORITE DISHES _____
_____
_____

NAME _____ PHONE _____
ADDRESS _____
HOURS _____ PRICE _____
FAVORITE DISHES _____
_____
_____

NAME _____ PHONE _____
ADDRESS _____
HOURS _____ PRICE _____
FAVORITE DISHES _____
_____
_____

NAME _____ PHONE _____

ADDRESS_____

HOURS _____ PRICE _____

FAVORITE DISHES _____

_____

_____

NAME _____ PHONE _____

ADDRESS_____

HOURS _____ PRICE _____

FAVORITE DISHES _____

_____

_____

NAME _____ PHONE _____

ADDRESS_____

HOURS _____ PRICE _____

FAVORITE DISHES _____

_____

_____

NAME _____ PHONE _____

ADDRESS_____

HOURS _____ PRICE _____

FAVORITE DISHES _____

_____

_____

NAME _____ PHONE _____

ADDRESS_____

HOURS _____ PRICE _____

FAVORITE DISHES _____

_____

_____

NAME _____ PHONE _____

ADDRESS_____

HOURS _____ PRICE _____

FAVORITE DISHES _____

_____

_____

NAME _____ PHONE _____

ADDRESS_____

HOURS _____ PRICE _____

FAVORITE DISHES _____

_____

_____

I think a delicately chosen, artfully presented, lingering, and languorous meal, indulged in publicly, can be one of the most successful fillips to a love affair, but only when it is done with some intelligence. The presence of the other near-invisible diners makes the promised isolation seem even more desirable. The waiters float in a conciliatory cloud. The food—but there is no need to give details of what in such an amorous pattern: almost anything in a good restaurant will be tinder to the flame, breath blown on the ash.

—M. F. K. FISHER, An Alphabet for Gourmets

NAME _____ PHONE _____

ADDRESS_____

HOURS _____ PRICE _____

FAVORITE DISHES _____

_____

_____

NAME _____ PHONE _____

ADDRESS_____

HOURS _____ PRICE _____

FAVORITE DISHES _____

_____

_____

NAME _____ PHONE _____

ADDRESS_____

HOURS _____ PRICE _____

FAVORITE DISHES _____

_____

_____

NAME _____ PHONE _____

ADDRESS_____

HOURS _____ PRICE _____

FAVORITE DISHES _____

_____

_____

NAME _____ PHONE _____

ADDRESS_____

HOURS _____ PRICE _____

FAVORITE DISHES _____

_____

_____

*Man does not live on what he eats but
on what he digests.*
—Alexander Dumas's Dictionary of Cuisine

NAME _____ PHONE _____

ADDRESS_____

HOURS _____ PRICE _____

FAVORITE DISHES _____

_____

_____

NAME _____ PHONE _____

ADDRESS_____

HOURS _____ PRICE _____

FAVORITE DISHES _____

_____

_____

NAME _____ PHONE _____

ADDRESS_____

HOURS _____ PRICE _____

FAVORITE DISHES _____

_____

_____

NAME _____ PHONE _____

ADDRESS_____

HOURS _____ PRICE _____

FAVORITE DISHES _____

_____

_____

NAME _____ PHONE _____

ADDRESS_____

HOURS _____ PRICE _____

FAVORITE DISHES _____

_____

_____

NAME _____ PHONE _____

ADDRESS_____

HOURS _____ PRICE _____

FAVORITE DISHES _____

_____

_____

NAME _____ PHONE _____

ADDRESS_____

HOURS _____ PRICE _____

FAVORITE DISHES _____

_____

_____

NAME _____ PHONE _____

ADDRESS_____

HOURS _____ PRICE _____

FAVORITE DISHES _____

_____

_____

NAME _____ PHONE _____

ADDRESS_____

HOURS _____ PRICE _____

FAVORITE DISHES _____

_____

_____

NAME _____ PHONE _____

ADDRESS_____

HOURS _____ PRICE _____

FAVORITE DISHES _____

_____

_____

NAME _____ PHONE _____

ADDRESS_____

HOURS _____ PRICE _____

FAVORITE DISHES _____

_____

_____

NAME _____ PHONE _____

ADDRESS_____

HOURS _____ PRICE _____

FAVORITE DISHES _____

_____

_____

Robert Jacquerez, 95, who dines daily at the Hôtel de France in Auch, contends that the key to living to such a ripe old age is balance: "Always drink as much mineral water as wine, always have a salad with your cassoulet, and always take bread with your foie gras."

—MAGGIE WALDRON, Cold Spaghetti at Midnight

NAME _____ PHONE _____

ADDRESS_____

HOURS _____ PRICE _____

FAVORITE DISHES _____

_____

_____

NAME _____ PHONE _____

ADDRESS_____

HOURS _____ PRICE _____

FAVORITE DISHES _____

_____

_____

NAME _____ PHONE _____
ADDRESS_____
HOURS _____ PRICE _____
FAVORITE DISHES _____
_____
_____

NAME _____ PHONE _____
ADDRESS_____
HOURS _____ PRICE _____
FAVORITE DISHES _____
_____
_____

NAME _____ PHONE _____
ADDRESS_____
HOURS _____ PRICE _____
FAVORITE DISHES _____
_____
_____

NAME _____ PHONE _____
ADDRESS_____
HOURS _____ PRICE _____
FAVORITE DISHES _____
_____
_____

One cannot think well, love well, sleep
well if one has not dined well.
—*VIRGINIA WOOLF*, A Room of One's Own

NAME _____ PHONE _____

ADDRESS_____

HOURS _____ PRICE _____

FAVORITE DISHES _____

_____

_____

NAME _____ PHONE _____

ADDRESS_____

HOURS _____ PRICE _____

FAVORITE DISHES _____

_____

_____

NAME _____ PHONE _____

ADDRESS_____

HOURS _____ PRICE _____

FAVORITE DISHES _____

_____

_____

NAME _____ PHONE _____

ADDRESS_____

HOURS _____ PRICE _____

FAVORITE DISHES _____

_____

_____

NAME _____ PHONE _____

ADDRESS_____

HOURS _____ PRICE _____

FAVORITE DISHES _____

_____

_____

grocery stores
& markets

BEST LOCAL MARKET

NAME _____ PHONE _____

ADDRESS _____

HOURS _____ MANAGER _____ PRICES _____

FRESH DELIVERY DAYS _____

SPECIALTIES _____

_____

BEST ETHNIC MARKET

NAME _____ PHONE _____

ADDRESS _____

HOURS _____ MANAGER _____ PRICES _____

SPECIALTIES _____

_____

BEST BREAD

NAME _____ PHONE _____

ADDRESS _____

HOURS _____ MANAGER _____ PRICES _____

SPECIALTIES _____

_____

BEST BAGELS

NAME _____ PHONE _____

ADDRESS _____

HOURS _____ MANAGER _____ PRICES _____

SPECIALTIES _____

_____

BEST PRODUCE

NAME _____ PHONE _____

ADDRESS _____

HOURS _____ MANAGER _____ PRICES _____

FRESH DELIVERY DAYS _____

SPECIALTIES _____

_____

BEST DAIRY PRODUCTS

NAME _____ PHONE _____

ADDRESS _____

HOURS _____ MANAGER _____ PRICES _____

SPECIALTIES/BRANDS_____

_____

_____

BEST DELICATESSEN

NAME _____ PHONE _____

ADDRESS _____

HOURS _____ MANAGER _____ PRICES _____

SPECIALTIES _____

_____

_____

BEST BUTCHER

NAME _____ PHONE _____

ADDRESS _____

HOURS _____ MANAGER _____ PRICES _____

SPECIALTIES _____

_____

BEST SEAFOOD

NAME _____ PHONE _____

ADDRESS _____

HOURS _____ MANAGER _____ PRICES _____

SPECIALTIES _____

_____

BEST COFFEE

NAME _____ PHONE _____

ADDRESS _____

HOURS _____ PRICES _____

SPECIALTIES/BRANDS/FLAVORS _____

_____

_____

BEST TEA

NAME _____ PHONE _____

ADDRESS _____

HOURS _____ PRICES _____

SPECIALTIES/BRANDS/FLAVORS _____

_____

_____

BEST WINE & SPIRITS

NAME _____ PHONE _____

ADDRESS _____

HOURS _____ PRICES _____

SPECIALTIES _____

_____

_____

BEST BEER

NAME _____ PHONE _____

ADDRESS _____

HOURS _____ PRICES _____

SPECIALTIES/BRANDS_____

_____

_____

cookware stores
& specialty shops

NAME _____ PHONE _____
ADDRESS_____
HOURS _____ PRICES _____
SPECIALTIES/BRANDS _____
_____
_____

NAME _____ PHONE _____
ADDRESS_____
HOURS _____ PRICES _____
SPECIALTIES/BRANDS _____
_____
_____

NAME _____ PHONE _____
ADDRESS_____
HOURS _____ PRICES _____
SPECIALTIES/BRANDS _____
_____
_____

NAME _____ PHONE _____
ADDRESS_____
HOURS _____ PRICES _____
SPECIALTIES/BRANDS _____
_____
_____

NAME _____ PHONE _____

ADDRESS_____

HOURS _____ PRICES _____

SPECIALTIES/BRANDS _____

_____

_____

NAME _____ PHONE _____

ADDRESS_____

HOURS _____ PRICES _____

SPECIALTIES/BRANDS _____

_____

_____

NAME _____ PHONE _____

ADDRESS_____

HOURS _____ PRICES _____

SPECIALTIES/BRANDS _____

_____

_____

NAME _____ PHONE _____

ADDRESS_____

HOURS _____ PRICES _____

SPECIALTIES/BRANDS _____

_____

_____

NAME _____ PHONE _____

ADDRESS_____

HOURS _____ PRICES _____

SPECIALTIES/BRANDS _____

_____

_____

where to find the best

ITEM	BRAND/SOURCE
Bread, French	
Bread, Italian	
Bread, specialty	
Cheeses, domestic	
Cheeses, French	
Cheeses, Italian	
Chicken, free-range	
Chicken, smoked	
Duck, fresh	
Duck, smoked	
Pasta, dry	
Pasta, fresh	
Olive oil, extra-virgin	
Oils (walnut, hazelnut, unrefined corn, etc.)	
Vinegar, balsamic	
Vinegar, other	
Mustard	
Tomatoes, in season	
Prosciutto, imported	
Sausages	
Ethnic ingredients, Mexican/Southwestern	
Ethnic ingredients, Thai	
Ethnic ingredients, Asian	

ITEM	BRAND/SOURCE
Ethnic ingredients, other	
Herbs, fresh	
Herbs & spices, dried	
Chocolate	
Vanilla & vanilla beans	
Flour	
Polenta	
Dried beans	
Rice	
Dried fruit	
Coffee	
Tea	
Wine, European	
Wine, California	
Wine, Oregon	
Wine, other	
Beer & ale	
Cookware	
Baking supplies	
Flowers	
Linens	

a well stocked Pantry

With a well stocked pantry you can rise to nearly any last-minute challenge, a stormy night, a cancelled date, or simply the desire to eat well while you hibernate for a few days. These basics will make all your cooking easier and more pleasant.

Kosher salt & whole black peppercorns & herbs & spices

Olive Oils

pure, for cooking
extra virgin, good commercial quality
extra virgin, condiment quality
(Tuscan or Luccese, Provencal, Ligurian, Californian)

Vinegars

Apple Cider, Red Wine (6 to 6.5% acidity);
Champagne (6 to 7% acidity) Raspberry (4.5% and 6 to 7% acidity); Rice Wine; Sherry, Balsamic

Mustards

Dijon; Coarse Grain; Coleman's
Dry Mustard Flour; Yellow Mustard Seed

Other Condiments

soy sauce, chutney, capers, green peppercorns; dried tomatoes in Olive Oil; Tabasco Sauce; honey; Sesame tahini

Dried Goods

Polenta, Stoneground Corn Meal, Cannellini Beans, Black beans, Pinto Beans; Wild Rice, Arborio Rice, Basmati Rice; Spaghetti, Linguine, Penne, Dried Tomato Bits, Yeast, Bread flour, Sugar

Canned Goods

Crushed Tomatoes; Whole Tomatoes; Tomato Paste in a tube; Anchovies; Brisling Sardines; Greek Olives; Green Olives; Tuna; Garbonza Beans; Chipotle Peppers; Chicken Broth, Coconut Milk

OPTIMUM STORAGE TIMES
OF COMMON STAPLES

Olive oil, pure	Cool, dark cupboard, up to 2 years
Olive oil, extra-virgin	Cool, dark cupboard, up to 6 months
Olive oil, flavored	Homemade: refrigerator, up to 1 week
	Purchased: cool, dark cupboard, up to 6 months
Walnut oil	Refrigerator, up to 4 months
Hazelnut oil	Refrigerator, up to 4 months
Vinegar	Cool, dark cupboard, up to 2 years
Vinegar, flavored	Cool, dark cupboard, up to 1 year
Mustard, flour	Cool, dark cupboard, up to 1 year
Mustard, prepared	Cool, dark cupboard, up to 3 months; refrigerator, up to 6 months
Mustard, flavored	Refrigerator, up to 6 months
Soy sauce	Cool, dark cupboard, up to 1 year
Dried tomatoes	Cool, dark cupboard, up to 6 months
Dried tomatoes, in oil	Refrigerator, up to 3 months
Polenta	Cool, dark cupboard, up to 6 months
Pasta, commercial dried	Cool, dark cupboard, up to 18 months
Rice, most types, including wild	Cool, dark cupboard, indefinitely
Rice, brown	Cool, dark cupboard for 1 month; refrigerator, up to 6 months
Flour, white	Cool, dark cupboard, up to 1 year
Flour, whole wheat	Cool, dark cupboard, 1 month; refrigerator, up to 1 year
Salt, all types	Indefinitely

Yeast	Fresh: refrigerator, up to 2 weeks
	Dry: cool, dark cupboard, until expiration date
Sugar, all types	Indefinitely
Honey	Cool, dark cupboard, up to 1 year
Spices	Cool, dark cupboard, up to 6 months; 1 year if whole
Tomatoes, canned	Cool, dark cupboard, up to 1 year
Onions	Cool, dark cupboard, up to 3 weeks; never with potatoes, not in plastic
Potatoes	Cool, dark cupboard (45–50°F), up to 2 months; never with onions, not in plastic
Garlic	Cool, dark cupboard, up to 3 months; never in refrigerator, not in plastic
Coffee, whole beans	Refrigerator, 1 month; freezer, 3 to 4 months
Tea, loose leaves or bagged	Cool, dark cupboard, up to 1 year
Chocolate	All types: cool, dark cupboard (under 70°F at all times)
	Dark: up to 1 year
	Milk: up to 6 months
Cocoa	Cool, dark cupboard, tightly sealed, up to 1 year
Walnuts	In shell: pantry, 2–3 months; refrigerator, up to 1 year
	Shelled: refrigerator, up to 1 year
Pinenuts	Refrigerator, up to 1 month
Pecans	In shell: pantry, 2–3 months; refrigerator, up to 6 months
	Shelled: refrigerator, up to 6 months
Almonds	In shell: pantry, 1 year
	Shelled: refrigerator, up to 6 months

USES FOR VINEGAR

TYPE OF VINEGAR	PRICE RANGE	RECOMMENDED USES
Balsamic, commercial	Inexpensive to expensive	Sauces, dressings, marinades, condiment
Balsamic, traditional	Extremely expensive	Condiment
Black	Inexpensive	Flavoring, Chinese and other Pacific Rim cuisines
Cane	Inexpensive	Philippine cuisine
Champagne	Moderate	Fruit vinegars, light dressings
Cider	Inexpensive to moderate	Preserves and chutneys
Distilled (white)	Inexpensive	Cleaning and general household uses
Malt	Inexpensive to moderate	Pickling, ketchup, fish and chips
Pineapple	Moderate	Dressings, salsas, flavoring
Raspberry	Moderate to expensive	Dressings, marinades, emulsions, flavoring, condiment
Red wine	Moderate	Hearty dressings, sauces, marinades, spice vinegars
Rice	Inexpensive to moderate	Thai and Japanese cuisine, with oysters, seafood
Sherry	Moderate to expensive	Sauces, soups, dressings
White wine	Moderate	Dressings, emulsions, herb vinegars, fruit vinegars

FATTY-ACID PROFILES OF COMMON CULINARY OILS
(percentages or parts per 100)

TYPE OF OIL	SATURATED FATTY ACIDS	MONO-UNSATURATED FATTY ACIDS	POLY-UNSATURATED FATTY ACIDS
Almond	9	65	26
Avocado	20	70	10
Canola (rapeseed)	6	60	34
Coconut	90	7.5	2.5
Corn	13	27	60
Cottonseed	24	26	50
Grapeseed	12	17	71
Hazelnut	10	76	14
Mustard	1	76	23
Olive	10	82	8
Peanut	17	61	22
Pumpkin seed	9	34	57
Rice bran	19	42	39
Safflower	6.6	16.4	77
Sesame	14	40	46
Soybean	14	24	62
Sunflower	13	21	66
Walnut	16	28	54

Sources: *Foods & Nutrition Encyclopedia,* 1983; *Composition of Foods,* 1963; *The Lipid Handbook,* 1986; *Spectrum Naturals Kitchen Guide,* 1990.

SMOKE POINTS OF COMMON CULINARY OILS

TYPE OF OIL	SMOKE POINT	SUITABLE COOKING METHODS OR USES
Almond	495°F	Dressings, grilled fish
Avocado	520°F	Dressings, too expensive for frying
Canola (rapeseed)	437°F	Frying, deep frying, sautéing
Coconut	Not available	Not recommended for cooking
Corn, refined	410°F	Frying, baking, sautéing
Corn, unrefined	250°F	Flavoring, dressings, emulsions
Cottonseed	450°F	Not recommended for cooking
Grapeseed	446°F	Deep-frying, frying, sautéing
Hazelnut	Not available	Dressings, sauces, flavoring
Mustard	Not available	Dressings, flavoring
Olive, extra-virgin	250°F	Dressings, flavoring, emulsions, condiment
Olive, pure refined	410°F	Frying, sautéing, baking
Peanut (ground nut)	450°F	Frying, deep-frying, emulsions, roux
Pumpkin seed	224°F	Dressings, flavoring
Rice bran	500°F	Too expensive for general use
Safflower	450°F	Deep-frying, frying
Sesame	410°F	Flavoring, stir-frying, sautéing
Soybean	450°F	Not recommended for frying: It foams at high temperatures
Sunflower	392°F	Frying, sautéing
Walnut	Not available	Dressings, sauces, flavoring, light sautéing

Sources: *Bailey's Industrial Oil & Fat Products,* 4th ed., 1979; and *Spectrum Natural Kitchen Guide,* 1990.

COMMERCIAL MUSTARDS

TYPE	CHARACTERISTICS	RECOMMENDED STORAGE	USES
Flour, mild (one of the standard retail dry mustards)	Pale yellow powder, heat on tongue	Pantry, well sealed against dampness	Mild homemade mustard; as a spice; pickling
Flour, hot (one of the standard retail dry mustards)	Deep yellow powder, full vaporizing heat	Pantry, well sealed against dampness	Chinese-style mustard; home-made mustards; as a spice in sauces, dressings; pickling
Colman's Dry	Mix of mild and hot mustard flours	Pantry, well sealed against dampness	English hot mustard; Chinese-style mustard; homemade mustards; as a spice in sauces, dressings; pickling
Seeds, white	Pale yellow seeds	Pantry, well sealed against dampness	Homemade coarse-grain mustard; pickling; Indian spice blends; garnish; sprouts
Seeds, brown	Tiny reddish black seeds	Pantry, well sealed against dampness	Homemade Dijon-style mustard; Indian spice blends; sprouts
American yellow	Sharply acidic but without much heat; made from white mustard seeds only	Refrigeration is not essential, but will help maintain maximum flavor	The basic hot-dog mustard
American brown	Mild with a bit of spiciness, less acidic than American yellow	Refrigeration is not essential, but will help maintain maximum flavor	As a condiment if you prefer a very mild mustard
English hot	Full taste on the tongue and full vaporization; very hot	Refrigeration is not essential, but will help maintain maximum flavor	As a condiment with smoked meats, Cheddar cheese, sausages, roast beef
Dijon	Typical Dijon that has been toned down some	Refrigeration is not essential, but will help maintain maximum flavor	As a condiment; in marinades, sauces, dressings

TYPE	CHARACTERISTICS	RECOMMENDED STORAGE	USES
Dijon, extra strong, for export	Smooth, suave, French mustard, more pungent than Dijon, but less so than that produced for domestic use (in France)	Refrigeration is not essential, but will help maintain maximum flavor	As a condiment; in marinades, sauces, dressings
Dijon, extra-forte, French	Smooth, suave, French mustard with full range of pungency	Refrigeration is not essential, but will help maintain maximum flavor	As a condiment; in marinades, sauces, dressings
Bordeaux	Made with whole brown seeds; sweet, spicy, tart	Pantry	As a condiment; on sandwiches, with smoked meats and pâtés
Meaux	Made with whole brown seeds; slightly spicy, very tart, not sweet	Pantry	As a condiment; on sandwiches, with smoked meats and pâtés
German hot	Brown, often hot, frequently sweet, and often flavored with horseradish	Refrigeration is not essential, but will help maintain maximum flavor	As a condiment with sausages, smoked meats, pâtés
Creole	Vary with producer, most often slightly coarse-grained brown mustard, rather tart	Refrigeration may not be essential, but will help maintain flavor; check ingredients list	As a condiment
Dijon-style	Many have an unpleasant floury texture; generally inferior in all ways to French mustards	Refrigeration is not essential, but will help maintain maximum flavor	Limited, unless you find one you particularly like
Flavored Dijon-style	Quality and characteristics vary greatly, as do flavors; those made with true Dijon tend to be best	Refrigeration often essential; check ingredients list	As a condiment
Other flavored mustards	Quality and characteristics vary greatly	Refrigeration often essential; check ingredients list	As a condiment

tasting notes

CHEESES

PARMIGIANO • FONTINA • GORGONZOLA • CHESHIRE • KASSERI •
JACK • BRIE • STILTON • CHÈVRE • CHEDDAR • SCHLOSS

TYPE _____ SOURCE COUNTRY/STATE _____

PLACE OF PURCHASE _____ COST _____ STORAGE REQUIREMENTS _____

APPEARANCE _____ AROMA _____ TEXTURE _____

TASTE _____ FINISH _____

BEST USES _____ WINE MATCH _____

NOTES _____

OVERALL OPINION _____ WILL PURCHASE AGAIN _____

TYPE _____ SOURCE COUNTRY/STATE _____

PLACE OF PURCHASE _____ COST _____ STORAGE REQUIREMENTS _____

APPEARANCE _____ AROMA _____ TEXTURE _____

TASTE _____ FINISH _____

BEST USES _____ WINE MATCH _____

NOTES _____

OVERALL OPINION _____ WILL PURCHASE AGAIN _____

TYPE _____ SOURCE COUNTRY/STATE _____

PLACE OF PURCHASE _____ COST _____ STORAGE REQUIREMENTS _____

APPEARANCE _____ AROMA _____ TEXTURE _____

TASTE _____ FINISH _____

BEST USES _____ WINE MATCH _____

NOTES _____

OVERALL OPINION _____ WILL PURCHASE AGAIN _____

TYPE _____ SOURCE COUNTRY/STATE _____

PLACE OF PURCHASE _____ COST _____ STORAGE REQUIREMENTS _____

APPEARANCE _____ AROMA _____ TEXTURE _____

TASTE _____ FINISH _____

BEST USES _____ WINE MATCH _____

NOTES _____

tasting notes

CHEESES

PARMIGIANO • FONTINA • GORGONZOLA • CHESHIRE • KASSERI •
JACK • BRIE • STILTON • CHÈVRE • CHEDDAR • SCHLOSS

TYPE _____ SOURCE COUNTRY/STATE _____

PLACE OF PURCHASE _____ COST _____ STORAGE REQUIREMENTS _____

APPEARANCE _____ AROMA _____ TEXTURE _____

TASTE _____ FINISH _____

BEST USES _____ WINE MATCH _____

NOTES _____

OVERALL OPINION _____ WILL PURCHASE AGAIN _____

TYPE _____ SOURCE COUNTRY/STATE _____

PLACE OF PURCHASE _____ COST _____ STORAGE REQUIREMENTS _____

APPEARANCE _____ AROMA _____ TEXTURE _____

TASTE _____ FINISH _____

BEST USES _____ WINE MATCH _____

NOTES _____

OVERALL OPINION _____ WILL PURCHASE AGAIN _____

TYPE _____ SOURCE COUNTRY/STATE _____

PLACE OF PURCHASE _____ COST _____ STORAGE REQUIREMENTS _____

APPEARANCE _____ AROMA _____ TEXTURE _____

TASTE _____ FINISH _____

BEST USES _____ WINE MATCH _____

NOTES _____

OVERALL OPINION _____ WILL PURCHASE AGAIN _____

TYPE _____ SOURCE COUNTRY/STATE _____

PLACE OF PURCHASE _____ COST _____ STORAGE REQUIREMENTS _____

APPEARANCE _____ AROMA _____ TEXTURE _____

TASTE _____ FINISH _____

BEST USES _____ WINE MATCH _____

NOTES _____

OVERALL OPINION _____ WILL PURCHASE AGAIN _____

tasting notes

MUSTARDS

DIJON • COARSE-GRAIN • ENGLISH • HOT & SWEET •
GERMAN • FLAVORED

BRAND NAME _____ SOURCE COUNTRY/STATE _____

PLACE OF PURCHASE _____ COST _____

COLOR/APPEARANCE _____ AROMA _____

TASTE _____ TEXTURE _____ CONSISTENCY _____

ACIDITY _____ BALANCE _____ FINISH _____

NOTES _____

OVERALL OPINION _____ WILL PURCHASE AGAIN _____

BRAND NAME _____ SOURCE COUNTRY/STATE _____

PLACE OF PURCHASE _____ COST _____

COLOR/APPEARANCE _____ AROMA _____

TASTE _____ TEXTURE _____ CONSISTENCY _____

ACIDITY _____ BALANCE _____ FINISH _____

NOTES _____

OVERALL OPINION _____ WILL PURCHASE AGAIN _____

BRAND NAME _____ SOURCE COUNTRY/STATE _____

PLACE OF PURCHASE _____ COST _____

COLOR/APPEARANCE _____ AROMA _____

TASTE _____ TEXTURE _____ CONSISTENCY _____

ACIDITY _____ BALANCE _____ FINISH _____

NOTES _____

OVERALL OPINION _____ WILL PURCHASE AGAIN _____

BRAND NAME _____ SOURCE COUNTRY/STATE _____

PLACE OF PURCHASE _____ COST _____

COLOR/APPEARANCE _____ AROMA _____

TASTE _____ TEXTURE _____ CONSISTENCY _____

ACIDITY _____ BALANCE _____ FINISH _____

NOTES _____

OVERALL OPINION _____ WILL PURCHASE AGAIN _____

tasting notes

MUSTARDS

DIJON • COARSE-GRAIN • ENGLISH • HOT & SWEET •
GERMAN • FLAVORED

BRAND NAME _____ SOURCE COUNTRY/STATE _____

PLACE OF PURCHASE _____ COST _____

COLOR/APPEARANCE _____ AROMA _____

TASTE _____ TEXTURE _____ CONSISTENCY _____

ACIDITY _____ BALANCE _____ FINISH _____

NOTES _____

OVERALL OPINION _____ WILL PURCHASE AGAIN _____

BRAND NAME _____ SOURCE COUNTRY/STATE _____

PLACE OF PURCHASE _____ COST _____

COLOR/APPEARANCE _____ AROMA _____

TASTE _____ TEXTURE _____ CONSISTENCY _____

ACIDITY _____ BALANCE _____ FINISH _____

NOTES _____

OVERALL OPINION _____ WILL PURCHASE AGAIN _____

BRAND NAME _____ SOURCE COUNTRY/STATE _____

PLACE OF PURCHASE _____ COST _____

COLOR/APPEARANCE _____ AROMA _____

TASTE _____ TEXTURE _____ CONSISTENCY _____

ACIDITY _____ BALANCE _____ FINISH _____

NOTES _____

OVERALL OPINION _____ WILL PURCHASE AGAIN _____

BRAND NAME _____ SOURCE COUNTRY/STATE _____

PLACE OF PURCHASE _____ COST _____

COLOR/APPEARANCE _____ AROMA _____

TASTE _____ TEXTURE _____ CONSISTENCY _____

ACIDITY _____ BALANCE _____ FINISH _____

NOTES _____

OVERALL OPINION _____ WILL PURCHASE AGAIN _____

137

tasting notes
HOMEGROWN TOMATOES
EARLY GIRL • BETTER BOY • MARVEL STRIPE • SWEET 100 •
BRANDYWINE • STUPICE • GREEN GRAPE • ENCHANTMENT

SEED TYPE/VARIETY _____ COLOR _____

SEED SOURCE _____ COST _____

DAYS TO MATURITY _____ APPEARANCE _____ WEIGHT _____

SKIN _____ TEXTURE _____ ACIDITY _____

SUGAR _____ TASTE _____

PROBLEMS/NOTES _____

OVERALL OPINION _____ WILL GROW AGAIN _____

SEED TYPE/VARIETY _____ COLOR _____

SEED SOURCE _____ COST _____

DAYS TO MATURITY _____ APPEARANCE _____ WEIGHT _____

SKIN _____ TEXTURE _____ ACIDITY _____

SUGAR _____ TASTE _____

PROBLEMS/NOTES _____

OVERALL OPINION _____ WILL GROW AGAIN _____

SEED TYPE/VARIETY _____ COLOR _____

SEED SOURCE _____ COST _____

DAYS TO MATURITY _____ APPEARANCE _____ WEIGHT _____

SKIN _____ TEXTURE _____ ACIDITY _____

SUGAR _____ TASTE _____

PROBLEMS/NOTES _____

OVERALL OPINION _____ WILL GROW AGAIN _____

SEED TYPE/VARIETY _____ COLOR _____

SEED SOURCE _____ COST _____

DAYS TO MATURITY _____ APPEARANCE _____ WEIGHT _____

SKIN _____ TEXTURE _____ ACIDITY _____

SUGAR _____ TASTE _____

PROBLEMS/NOTES _____

OVERALL OPINION _____ WILL GROW AGAIN _____

tasting notes

Homegrown Tomatoes

Early Girl • Better Boy • Marvel Stripe • Sweet 100 •
Brandywine • Stupice • Green Grape • Enchantment

SEED TYPE/VARIETY _____ COLOR _____

SEED SOURCE _____ COST _____

DAYS TO MATURITY _____ APPEARANCE _____ WEIGHT _____

SKIN _____ TEXTURE _____ ACIDITY _____

SUGAR _____ TASTE _____

PROBLEMS/NOTES _____

OVERALL OPINION _____ WILL GROW AGAIN _____

SEED TYPE/VARIETY _____ COLOR _____

SEED SOURCE _____ COST _____

DAYS TO MATURITY _____ APPEARANCE _____ WEIGHT _____

SKIN _____ TEXTURE _____ ACIDITY _____

SUGAR _____ TASTE _____

PROBLEMS/NOTES _____

OVERALL OPINION _____ WILL GROW AGAIN _____

SEED TYPE/VARIETY _____ COLOR _____

SEED SOURCE _____ COST _____

DAYS TO MATURITY _____ APPEARANCE _____ WEIGHT _____

SKIN _____ TEXTURE _____ ACIDITY _____

SUGAR _____ TASTE _____

PROBLEMS/NOTES _____

OVERALL OPINION _____ WILL GROW AGAIN _____

SEED TYPE/VARIETY _____ COLOR _____

SEED SOURCE _____ COST _____

DAYS TO MATURITY _____ APPEARANCE _____ WEIGHT _____

SKIN _____ TEXTURE _____ ACIDITY _____

SUGAR _____ TASTE _____

PROBLEMS/NOTES _____

OVERALL OPINION _____ WILL GROW AGAIN _____

SOURCE COUNTRY _____ BRAND NAME _____

PLACE OF PURCHASE _____ PRICE _____

COLOR/APPEARANCE _____ AROMA _____

CONSISTENCY _____ TASTE _____ FINISH _____

NOTES _____

_____

OVERALL OPINION _____ WILL PURCHASE AGAIN _____

SOURCE COUNTRY _____ BRAND NAME _____

PLACE OF PURCHASE _____ PRICE _____

COLOR/APPEARANCE _____ AROMA _____

CONSISTENCY _____ TASTE _____ FINISH _____

NOTES _____

_____

OVERALL OPINION _____ WILL PURCHASE AGAIN _____

SOURCE COUNTRY _____ BRAND NAME _____

PLACE OF PURCHASE _____ PRICE _____

COLOR/APPEARANCE _____ AROMA _____

CONSISTENCY _____ TASTE _____ FINISH _____

NOTES _____

_____

OVERALL OPINION _____ WILL PURCHASE AGAIN _____

SOURCE COUNTRY _____ BRAND NAME _____

PLACE OF PURCHASE _____ PRICE _____

COLOR/APPEARANCE _____ AROMA _____

CONSISTENCY _____ TASTE _____ FINISH _____

NOTES _____

_____

OVERALL OPINION _____ WILL PURCHASE AGAIN _____

tasting notes

Extra-Virgin Olive Oils

SOURCE COUNTRY _____ BRAND NAME _____ _____

PLACE OF PURCHASE _____ PRICE _____

COLOR/APPEARANCE _____ AROMA _____

CONSISTENCY _____ TASTE _____ FINISH _____

NOTES _____

_____

OVERALL OPINION _____ WILL PURCHASE AGAIN _____

SOURCE COUNTRY _____ BRAND NAME _____

PLACE OF PURCHASE _____ PRICE _____

COLOR/APPEARANCE _____ AROMA _____

CONSISTENCY _____ TASTE _____ FINISH _____

NOTES _____

_____

OVERALL OPINION _____ WILL PURCHASE AGAIN _____

SOURCE COUNTRY _____ BRAND NAME _____

PLACE OF PURCHASE _____ PRICE _____

COLOR/APPEARANCE _____ AROMA _____

CONSISTENCY _____ TASTE _____ FINISH _____

NOTES _____

_____

OVERALL OPINION _____ WILL PURCHASE AGAIN _____

SOURCE COUNTRY _____ _____ BRAND NAME _____ _____

PLACE OF PURCHASE _____ PRICE _____

COLOR/APPEARANCE _____ AROMA ___ _____

CONSISTENCY _____ TASTE _____ FINISH _____

NOTES _____

_____

OVERALL OPINION _____ WILL PURCHASE AGAIN _____

tasting notes
VINEGARS
RED WINE • WHITE WINE • CHAMPAGNE • SHERRY • RASPBERRY •
FRUIT • HERB • BALSAMIC • MALT • CIDER

TYPE OF VINEGAR _____ PLACE OF PURCHASE _____

BRAND _____ COST _____ ACIDITY (GRAIN) _____

COLOR _____ CLARITY _____ AROMA (BOUQUET) _____

BODY_____TASTE _____

BEST USES _____

NOTES _____

OVERALL OPINION _____ WILL PURCHASE AGAIN _____

TYPE OF VINEGAR _____ PLACE OF PURCHASE _____

BRAND _____ COST _____ ACIDITY (GRAIN) _____

COLOR _____ CLARITY _____ AROMA (BOUQUET) _____

BODY_____TASTE _____

BEST USES _____

NOTES _____

OVERALL OPINION _____ WILL PURCHASE AGAIN _____

TYPE OF VINEGAR _____ PLACE OF PURCHASE _____

BRAND _____ COST _____ ACIDITY (GRAIN) _____

COLOR _____ CLARITY _____ AROMA (BOUQUET) _____

BODY_____TASTE _____

BEST USES _____

NOTES _____

OVERALL OPINION _____ WILL PURCHASE AGAIN _____

TYPE OF VINEGAR _____ PLACE OF PURCHASE _____

BRAND _____ COST _____ ACIDITY (GRAIN) _____

COLOR _____ CLARITY _____ AROMA (BOUQUET) _____

BODY_____TASTE _____

BEST USES _____

NOTES _____

OVERALL OPINION _____ WILL PURCHASE AGAIN _____

tasting notes

VINEGARS

RED WINE • WHITE WINE • CHAMPAGNE • SHERRY • RASPBERRY •
FRUIT • HERB • BALSAMIC • MALT • CIDER

TYPE OF VINEGAR _____ PLACE OF PURCHASE _____

BRAND _____ COST _____ ACIDITY (GRAIN) _____

COLOR _____ CLARITY _____ AROMA (BOUQUET) _____

BODY_____TASTE _____

BEST USES _____

NOTES _____

OVERALL OPINION _____ WILL PURCHASE AGAIN _____

TYPE OF VINEGAR _____ PLACE OF PURCHASE _____

BRAND _____ COST _____ ACIDITY (GRAIN) _____

COLOR _____ CLARITY _____ AROMA (BOUQUET) _____

BODY_____TASTE _____

BEST USES _____

NOTES _____

OVERALL OPINION _____ WILL PURCHASE AGAIN _____

TYPE OF VINEGAR _____ PLACE OF PURCHASE _____

BRAND _____ COST _____ ACIDITY (GRAIN) _____

COLOR _____ CLARITY _____ AROMA (BOUQUET) _____

BODY_____TASTE _____

BEST USES _____

NOTES _____

OVERALL OPINION _____ WILL PURCHASE AGAIN _____

TYPE OF VINEGAR _____ PLACE OF PURCHASE _____

BRAND _____ COST _____ ACIDITY (GRAIN) _____

COLOR _____ CLARITY _____ AROMA (BOUQUET) _____

BODY_____TASTE _____

BEST USES _____

NOTES _____

OVERALL OPINION _____ WILL PURCHASE AGAIN _____

TABLES OF EQUIVALENTS

OVEN TEMPERATURES

CASUAL	FAHRENHEIT	CELSIUS	GAS
Very slow	250	121	1/2
Very slow	275	135	1
Slow	300	148	2
Moderate	325	163	3
Moderate	350	177	4
Moderate	375	190	5
Hot	400	204	6
Hot	425	218	7
Hot	450	232	8
Very hot	475	246	9
Very hot	500	260	10

U.S./U.K.	METRIC
oz = ounce	g = gram
lb = pound	kg = kilogram
in = inch	mm = millimeter
ft = foot	cm = centimeter
tsp = teaspoon	ml = milliliter
tbl = tablespoon	l = liter
fl oz = fluid ounce	
qt = quart	

LIQUID MEASURES

FLUID OUNCES	U.S. MEASURES	IMPERIAL MEASURE	METRIC
	1 tsp	1 tsp	5 ml
$1/4$	2 tsp	1 dessertspoon	7 ml
$1/2$	1 tbl	1 tbl	15 ml
1	2 tbl	2 tbl	28 ml
2	$1/4$ cup	4 tbl	56 ml
4	$1/2$ cup ($1/4$ pint)		110 ml
5		$1/4$ pint/1 gill	140 ml
6	$3/4$ cup		170 ml
8	1 cup ($1/2$ pint)		225 ml
9			250 ml ($1/4$ liter)
10	$1^1/4$ cups	$1/2$ pint	280 ml
12	$1^1/2$ cups ($3/4$ pint)		340 ml
15		$3/4$ pint	420 ml
16	2 cups (1 pint)		450 ml
18	$2^1/3$ cups		500 ml ($1/2$ liter)
20	$2^1/2$ cups	1 pint	560 ml
24	3 cups ($1^1/2$ pints)		675 ml
25		$1^1/4$ pints	700 ml
27	$3^1/2$ cups		750 ml
30	$3^3/4$ cups	$1^1/2$ pints	840 ml
32	4 cups (1 quart)		900 ml
35		$1^3/4$ pints	980 ml
36	$4^1/2$ cups		1000 ml (1 liter)
128	1 gallon	32 gills	3785 ml
	(4 quarts, 16 cups)		(3.75 liters)

SOLID MEASURES

U.S./U.K. OUNCES	U.S./U.K. POUNDS	GRAMS	KILOS
1		28	
2		56	
$3^1/2$		100	
4	$1/4$	112	
5		140	
6		168	
8	$1/2$	225	
9		250	$1/4$
12	$3/4$	340	
16	1	450	
18		500	$1/2$
20	$1^1/4$	560	
24	$1^1/2$	675	
27		750	$3/4$
28	$1^3/4$	780	
32	2	900	
36	$2^1/4$	1000	1

Equivalents of Common Pantry Staples

WHITE SUGAR
1/4 cup/2 oz/60 g
1/3 cup/3 oz/75 g
1/2 cup/4 oz/125 g
3/4 cup/6 oz/185 g
1 cup/8 oz/250 g

BROWN SUGAR
1/4 cup/1 1/2 oz/45 g
1/2 cup/3 oz/90 g
3/4 cup/4 oz/125 g
1 cup/5 1/2 oz/170 g
1 1/2 cups/8 oz/250 g

POLENTA/CORNMEAL/
LONG-GRAIN RICE
1/3 cup/2 oz/60 g
1/2 cup/2 1/2 oz/75 g
3/4 cup/4 oz/125 g
1 cup/5 oz/155 g
1 1/2 cups/8 oz/250 g

DRIED BEANS
1/4 cup/1 1/2 oz/45 g
1/3 cup/2 oz/60 g
1/2 cup/3 oz/90 g
3/4 cup/5 oz/155 g
1 cup/6 oz/185g
1 1/2 cups/8 oz/250 g

ALL PURPOSE FLOUR/DRIED
BREAD CRUMBS/CHOPPED NUTS
1/4 cup/1 oz/30 g
1/3 cup/1 1/2 oz/45 g
1/2 cup/2 oz/60 g
3/4 cup/3 oz/90 g

1 cup/4 oz/125 g
1 1/2 cups/6 oz/185 g
2 cups/8 oz/250 g

WHOLE-WHEAT FLOUR
3 tbl/1 oz/30 g
1/2 cup/2 oz/60 g
2/3 cup/3 oz/90 g
1 cup/4 oz/125 g
1 1/4 cups/5 oz/155 g
1 2/3 cups/7 oz/210 g
1 3/4 cups/8 oz/250 g

HONEY
2 tbl/2 oz/60 g
1/4 cup/3 oz/90 g
1/2 cup/5 oz/155 g
3/4 cup/8 oz/250 g
1 cup/11 oz/345 g

GRATED HARD CHEESE
(PARMIGIANO/ROMANO/DRY JACK)
1/4 cup/1 oz/30 g
1/2 cup/2 oz/60 g
3/4 cup/3 oz/90 g
1 cup/4 oz/125 g
1 1/3 cups/5 oz/155 g
2 cups/7 oz/220 g

BUTTER (AND OTHER SOLID FATS)
1 tbl/1/2 oz/15 g
2 tbl/1 oz/30 g
4 tbl/2 oz/60 g
8 tbl/4 oz/115 g (1 stick, 1/2 cup)
16 tbl/8 oz/225 g (2 sticks, 1 cup)
32 tbl/16 oz/450 g (4 sticks, 2 cups)

the good cook's
basic recipes

CROUTONS • COURT BOUILLON • VEGETABLE BROTH • POULTRY STOCK •

MEAT STOCK • FISH FUMET • ROASTED GARLIC • ROASTED-GARLIC PURÉE

● To make croutons, place about ¾ cup of extra-virgin olive oil in a large jar that has a lid. Add 4 cups of cubed sourdough bread, close the container, and shake it until the bread has absorbed all the oil and the cubes are evenly coated. Add 1 teaspoon kosher salt and 2 teaspoons freshly ground pepper, shake again, and then place the cubes on a baking sheet and bake in a 250°F oven until the croutons are golden and dry. Cool, use immediately, or store in an airtight container.

● To make court bouillon for poaching fish, in a fish-poaching pan or other large container with a rack place 1 quart water; ½ bottle dry white wine; ½ cup cider vinegar; ½ lemon, quartered; a large carrot, cut in chunks; 2 large yellow onions, cut in quarters; 1 medium leek, trimmed and cut in chunks; 3 sprigs of Italian parsley; 2 sprigs of fresh thyme; 1 bay leaf; and 1 tablespoon kosher salt. Set the rack on top of the vegetables, bring the mixture to a boil, and lower the heat. Place the fish on the rack and poach it until it flakes easily. To preserve the liquid after poaching, strain it and store it in the refrigerator for up to three days. To reuse, extend it with additional water or wine.

● To make vegetable broth, cut 2 peeled carrots, 4 onions, 4 trimmed leeks, 1 rib of celery, 1 fennel bulb, and—if in season—1 large tomato into chunks. Place them in a heavy roasting pan, toss with just enough olive oil to coat them, and roast in a 325°F oven for 45 minutes, until they are tender and beginning to color. Remove them from the oven, place in a large, heavy pot, and add 3 quarts of fresh cold water. Add 4 trimmed scallions, and a few sprigs of Italian parsley, thyme, oregano, and marjoram and bring to a boil. Skim thoroughly, lower the heat, and simmer for 2 hours. Strain the broth and store it in the refrigerator or freezer until ready to use. This recipe makes approximately $2\frac{1}{2}$ quarts (10 cups).

● To make poultry stock, place 5 pounds of poultry parts—any combination of backs, necks, meaty carcasses, and wings—in a large heavy pot. Add 5 quarts water, bring to a boil, skim, and reduce to a simmer. Meanwhile, cut 1 medium yellow onion, 1 peeled medium carrot, 1 rib of celery, and 1 trimmed leek into chunks. Place them in a roasting pan, toss with enough olive oil to coat them, and roast in a 325°F oven for 45 minutes, until they are tender and beginning to color. Remove them from the oven and add them to the poultry stock. Simmer, partially covered, for about 3 hours, until the liquid is reduced by half. Let the stock cool, strain it, then refrigerate it, covered, or freeze it until ready to use. Before using the stock, remove and discard the fat.

● To make simple meat stock, cut 3 pounds of lean beef into large chunks and sauté it in a large, heavy pot until it begins to brown. Add 2 or 3 pounds marrow bones and 3 quarts fresh cold water. Bring the stock to a boil, reduce the heat to a simmer, skim off any scum that forms, and cook, uncovered, for 45 minutes. Meanwhile, cut 1 medium yellow onion, 1 peeled medium carrot, 1 rib of celery, 1 trimmed leek, and 3 large tomatoes into chunks. Place them in a roasting pan, toss with enough olive oil to coat them, and roast in a 325°F oven for 45 minutes, until they are tender and beginning to color. Remove them from the oven and add them to the meat stock, along with several sprigs of Italian parsley and 1 tablespoon black peppercorns. Continue to simmer, partially covered, for 2 hours. Cool the stock, strain it, and refrigerate or freeze it. Remove the fat before using the stock.

● To make fish fumet, place 3 pounds fish heads and bones (without skins), 1 large quartered yellow onion, 2 or 3 sprigs Italian parsley, 1 bay leaf, $\frac{1}{2}$ lemon, 1 cup dry white wine, 1 teaspoon black peppercorns, and 4 cups water in a large soup kettle. Bring the mixture to a boil, reduce the heat, skim off any scum that forms, and simmer for 30 minutes. Strain the stock, cool it, and refrigerate it for up to 3 days. You may also freeze fish stock. As a substitute for true stock, use a mixture of 2 parts clam juice, 1 part white wine, 1 part water, and the juice of 1 lemon.

● To make roasted garlic, clean 2 or 3 heads of raw garlic, leaving the bulb intact but removing any dirt that may cling to the roots and as much of the dry outer skin as will come off easily. Place the bulbs in a small ovenproof dish or pan, add about $1/2$ cup olive oil and $1/4$ cup water, season with salt and pepper, cover, and bake at 325°F for 45 to 60 minutes, until the garlic is the consistency of soft butter. Remove the garlic from the oven and let it cool on absorbent paper. Serve with bread and, if you wish, cream cheese or fresh goat cheese.

● To make roasted-garlic purée, when the roasted garlic (see preceding recipe) has cooled enough to be easy to handle, set it on a cutting board, remove the root, and use the heel of your hand to press out the pulp. If necessary, squeeze the pulp out clove by clove. Scrape the pulp off the cutting board, place it in a small bowl, and mash it with a fork until it is smooth. An average head of garlic will yield approximately 2 tablespoons of purée.

HOW TO COOK RICE & GRAINS

To serve a simple rice or grain accompaniment, follow these basic guidelines. In all cases, add a teaspoon of salt to the cooking water. In addition, other liquids such as stock or part stock and part water may be used. Consult specific recipes for such changes. Unless otherwise indicated, all grains should cook at a light simmer over low to medium-low heat.

GRAIN	QUANTITY	LIQUID	COOKING TIME	YIELD/PORTION
Rice, long grain	1 cup	$1^2/_3$ cup cold water	20 minutes, tightly covered, low heat; let rest 10 minutes after cooking	3 cups/ 6 servings
Rice, Basmati	1 cup, rinsed	2 cups cold water	20 minutes, tightly covered, low heat; let rest 10 minutes after cooking	3 cups/ 6 servings
Rice, brown	1 cup	$2^1/_2$ cups boiling water	40 to 50 minutes, covered	3 to 4 cups/ 6 to 8 servings
Rice, wild	1 cup, rinsed	4 cups cold water	45 minutes, covered	$3^1/_2$ to 4 cups/ 6 to 8 servings
Polenta	1 cup	4 cups cold water	20–40 minutes, uncovered; stir frequently	$3^1/_2$ to 4 cups/ 4 to 6 servings
Polenta	1 cup	4 cups boiling water	$1^1/_2$ hours, covered, in a double boiler over low heat; stir occasionally	$3^1/_2$ to 4 cups/ 4 to 6 servings
Polenta	1 cup	4 cups boiling water, plus 2 tablespoons butter	Bake at 350°F for 40 minutes, stir, bake additional 10 minutes	$3^1/_2$ to 4 cups/ 4 to 6 servings
Hominy grits	1 cup	4 cups boiling water	30 minutes, uncovered, stir occasionally	$3^1/_2$ to 4 cups/ 4 to 6 servings
Quinoa	1 cup, rinsed	2 cups cold water	12 to 15 minutes, covered	3 cups/ 4 to 6 servings

THE GOOD COOK'S SOURCES

ART OF EATING, THE
Box 242
Peacham, VT 05862
Culinary periodical.

BALDUCCI'S
424 Sixth Avenue
New York, NY 10011
(212) 673-2600
Excellent selection of Italian imports, including vinegars, beans, flours, and cheeses. Will ship.

BANDON CHAMBER OF COMMERCE
Bandon, OR
(503) 347-9616
Information on the Bandon Cranberry Festival, held early each fall.

BANGKOK GROCERY
1021 West Lawrence
Chicago, IL 60640
(312) 784-0001
(312) 784-2904
Mail-order source for Thai products, including chilies, lemongrass, and kaffir lime leaves.

BAT CONSERVATION INTERNATIONAL
P. O. Box 162603
Austin, TX 78716-2603
(512) 327-9721
Everything you might want to know about bats, bat houses, and more, with a beautiful newsletter for members.

BATON ROUGE CRAWFISH COMPANY
9121 Amber Drive
Baton Rouge, LA 70809
(504) 756-4807
Mail-order source for crawfish.

BELZONI-HUMPHREYS COUNTY
INDUSTRIAL DEVELOPMENT
FOUNDATION, INC.
528 North Hayden Street
Belzoni, MS
(601) 247-4238
Information about the World Catfish Festival.

BLAND FARMS
P. O. Box 506
Glennville, GA 30427
(800) VIDALIA
One of the largest growers and shippers of Vidalia onions. Catalog.

BOOKS FOR COOKS
301 South Light Street
Baltimore, MD 21202
(410) 547-9066

CAFÉ BEAUJOLAIS BAKERY
P. O. Box 730-M
Mendocino, CA 95460
(707) 937-5614
Specialty baked goods and other products from the well-known restaurant are available by mail. Catalog.

CALIFORNIA TOMATO BOARD
2017 North Gateway, Suite 102
Fresno, CA 93727
(800) 827-0628
Consumer information on California tomatoes.

CALIFORNIA TOMATO GROWERS
ASSOCIATION
P. O. Box 7398
Stockton, CA 95267
(209) 478-1761
Consumer information on tomatoes.

CAPERS STORE & COURTYARD CAFE
2285 West 4th Avenue
Vancouver, British Columbia V6J 1N3
(604) 739-6646 (store)
(604) 739-6685 (restaurant)
*Organic and health-food grocery store with a
restaurant.*

CASTROVILLE ARTICHOKE FESTIVAL
P. O. Box 1041
Castroville, CA 95012
(408) 633-CHOK
Information about the festival.

CHILE SHOP, THE
109 East Water Street
Sante Fe, NM 87501
(505) 983-6080
(505) 984-0737
*Mail-order source for all types of chilies, ristras,
blue corn products, and more. Catalog.*

CHIPPOKES PLANTATION STATE PARK
Route 1, Box 213
Surry, VA 23883
(804) 294-3625
*Information regarding the Pork, Peanut, and
Pine Festival.*

CHOCOLATE ARTS
2037 West 4th Avenue
Vancouver, British Columbia V6J 1N3
(604) 739-0475
*Exquisite chocolates made with organic ingredi-
ents; some of the molds are designed by Haida
artist Robert Davidson.*

CHOCOLATE MOUSSE KITCHENWARE
1553 Robson Street
Vancouver, British Columbia V6G 1C3
(604) 682-8223
Kitchenware, giftware, and cookbooks.

COASTAL COOKBOOK COMPANY
114D 2187 Oak Bay Avenue
Victoria, British Columbia V8R 1G1
(604) 595-5208
General cookbook store.

CODY'S BOOKS
Telegraph Avenue
Berkeley, CA
(800) 479-7744
*General bookstore with large culinary section.
Mail-order.*

COMPLEAT COOK
10816 MacLeod Trail South
294 Willopark Village
Calgary, Alberta T2J 5N8
(403) 278-1220

COOK'S BOOK SHOP, THE
3854 Fifth Avenue
San Diego, CA 92103
(619) 295-3636

COOK'S LIBRARY, THE
8373 West Third Street
Los Angeles, CA 90048
(213) 655-3141

COOKBOOK COMPANY
880 16th Avenue S.W.
Calgary, Alberta T2R 1J9
(403) 228-6066
*General cookbook store; mail-order catalog
available.*

COOKBOOK COTTAGE
1279 Bardstown Road
Louisville, KY 40204
(502) 458-5227

COOKBOOK STORE, THE
850 Young Street
Toronto, Ontario M4W 2HI
(416) 920-2665

CORTI BROTHERS
5810 Folsom Boulevard
Sacramento, CA 95819
(916) 736-3800
Excellent array of extra-virgin olive oils, authentic balsamic vinegars, and other Italian products. Will ship.

COYOTE CAFE GENERAL STORE
132 West Water Street
Santa Fe, NM 87501
(505) 982-2454
Mail-order source for various Southwestern ingredients, including chilies, beans, nuts, tamarinds, chocolate, masa harina, and 200 hot sauces. Catalog.

CRANBERRY INSTITUTE
P. O. Box 535
East Wareham, MA 02538
(508) 295-4895
All manner of information on cranberries. Newsletter for members.

CRAWFISH RESEARCH AND PROMOTION BOARD
P. O. Box 3334
Baton Rouge, LA 70821-3334
(504) 922-1280
Consumer information on crawfish.

D'ARTAGNAN, INC.
399-419 St. Paul Avenue
Jersey City, NJ 07306
(800) 327-8246
Excellent source for sausages, confit, foie gras, and game. Catalog.

DEAN & DELUCA
110 Greene Street, Suite 304
New York, NY 10012
(212) 254-8776
Outstanding selection of imported cheeses, condiments, oils, vinegars, olives, beans, grains, flours, rices, and more, as well as cookbooks, equipment (including food mills and potato ricers), and other culinary paraphernalia. Will ship.

DRAEGER'S MARKET & CULINARY CENTER
1010 University Drive
Menlo Park, CA 94026
(415) 688-0677
Full-service market, café, and cookware store. Excellent cookbook selection and outstanding cooking classes.

DUBRULLE FRENCH CULINARY SCHOOL
1522 West 8th Avenue
Vancouver, British Columbia V6J 4R8
(604) 738-3155
Year-round cooking school specializing in French cuisine; offers professional culinary training as well as a professional pastry and desserts program.

EXECUTIVE CHEF
1780 West 3rd Avenue
Vancouver, British Columbia V6J 1K4
(604) 731-3663
Food store specializing in high-end cookbooks, European foods, and elegant take-out foods.

FLORIDA TOMATO COMMITTEE
P. O. Box 140635
Orlando, FL 32814
(407) 894-3071
Consumer information on Florida tomatoes.

FOOD HISTORY NEWS
HCR 81, Box 354A
Islesboro, ME 04848
Culinary periodical.

G & R FARMS
Route 3, Box 35A
Glennville, GA 30427
(800) 522-0567
Vidalia onion farmers since 1945. Catalog; mail order.

G. B. RATTO, INTERNATIONAL
GROCERS
821 Washington Street
Oakland, CA 94607
(510) 832-6503
Excellent source for grains, beans, flours, vinegars, olive oils, French butter, spices, and more. Will ship. Catalog.

GILROY GARLIC FESTIVAL
P. O. Box 2311
Gilroy, CA 95020
(408) 842-1625
Information on the largest of the country's garlic festivals.

GUMBO FESTIVAL
P. O. Box 7069
Bridge City, LA 70094
Information on the festival.

HAUTE CUISINE
1210 Broad Street
Victoria, British Columbia V8W 2A4
(604) 388-9906

HERITAGE SEED PROGRAM
Route 3
Uxbridge, Ontario L9P 1R3
Membership, $18.00 U.S., $15.00 Can.
Canada's version of Seed Savers Exchange.

INTERNATIONAL BANANA FESTIVAL
P. O. Box 428
Fulton, KY 42041
Information about the festival.

INTERNATIONAL OLIVE OIL COUNCIL
P. O. Box 2197, J. A. F. Station
New York, NY 10116
Consumer information.

INTERNATIONAL PINOT NOIR FESTIVAL
P. O. Box 1310
McMinnville, OR 97128
(800) 775-4762
Information on the festival.

JOHNNY'S SELECTED SEEDS
310 Foss Hill Road
Albion, ME 04910
(207) 437-9294
Catalog, free.

JOSIE'S BEST
P. O. Box 5525
Santa Fe, NM 87502
(505) 473-3437
Mail-order source for Southwestern products, including posole, frozen chilies, and chili powder. Catalog.

KAM MAN FOOD PRODUCTS
200 Canal Street
New York, NY 10013
(212) 571-0330
(212) 766-9085
Thai products.

KERMIT LYNCH WINE MERCHANT
1605 San Pablo Avenue
Berkeley, CA 94702-1317
(510) 524-1524
Excellent source for French and Italian wines, plus a limited but choice selection of food products, including the best Dijon mustard, anchovies in olive oil, olives, tapenade, lavender honey, and extra-virgin olive oils from Provence, Tuscany, and Liguria. Newsletter, too.

KING ARTHUR FLOUR
The Baker's Catalogue
Route 2, Box 56
Norwich, VT 05055
(800) 827-6836
Grains, flours, other ingredients, and equipment for the home baker.

KITCHEN ARTS & LETTERS
1435 Lexington Avenue
New York, NY 10128
(212) 876-5550
A bookstore devoted exclusively to food and wine. Mail and phone orders.

KOBAYASHI SHOTEN
Japanese & Oriental Grocery
1518 Robson Street
Vancouver, British Columbia V6G 1C2
(604) 683-1019 (fax also)
Specializes in Japanese food but also carries supplies for other oriental cuisines.

KOOTENAY COOP
295 Baker Street
Nelson, British Columbia V1L 4H4
(604) 354-4077
Health foods, organic produce, locally made breads and chocolate.

LAURA CHENEL'S CHÈVRE
4310 Fremont Drive
Sonoma, CA 95476
(707) 996-4477
Selection of excellent French-style goat cheeses, fresh and aged, available by mail order.

LEBANON/MARION COUNTY
CHAMBER OF COMMERCE
107A West Main Street
Lebanon, KY 40033
(502) 692-2661
Information regarding Ham Days.

MAID OF SCANDINAVIA
3244 Raleigh Avenue
Minneapolis, MN 55416
(800) 328-6722
Everything for the home baker, from chocolate molds, butter molds, and candy-making equipment to colored candy foils, doilies, quality chocolate, powdered food coloring, copper bowls for Kitchen Aid mixers, and much more. Catalog.

MAISON GLASS
111 East 58th Street
New York, NY 10022-1211
(212) 755-3316
Mail-order source for fresh truffles.

MANICARETTI IMPORTS
299 Lawrence Avenue
South San Francisco, CA 94080
(415) 589-1120
(415) 589-5766 fax
Importers of outstanding Italian polenta and a wealth of other products, including olives, olive pastes, and extra-virgin olive oils. Fax for a list of locations near you that carry the products.

McCOY'S COOKWARE
2759 4th Street
Santa Rosa, CA 95405
(707) 526-3856
Best California cookware store north of San Francisco.

MONTERREY FOODS
3939 Brooklyn
Los Angeles, CA 90063
(213) 263-2143
Southwestern and Mexican food products. Mail order.

MOUNT HOREB MUSTARD MUSEUM
109 East Main Street
Mount Horeb, WI 53572
(608) 437-3986
Food emporium with a display collection of over 2,000 mustards. Hundreds for sale, along with mustard paraphernalia, T-shirts, books, and a newsletter. Catalog.

MOZZARELLA COMPANY
2944 Elm Street
Dallas, TX 75226
(214) 741-4072
(214) 741-4076 fax
Fresh and aged cheeses, including sheep's milk pecorino, fresh and smoked mozzarella, and taleggio from Paul Lambert. Will ship.

NAPA VALLEY MUSTARD FESTIVAL
P. O. Box 3603
Yountville, CA 94599
(707) 259-9020
Information on a month's worth of events.

NELLIE & JOE'S, INC.
P. O. Box 2368
Key West, FL 33045
(305) 296-5566
Mail-order (prepaid) source for authentic Key lime juice.

NORTH AMERICAN TRUFFLING SOCIETY
P. O. Box 269
Corvallis, OR 97339
(503) 752-2243
Organization of truffle aficionados.

NORTHERN CALIFORNIA OLIVE OIL COUNCIL
P. O. Box 675
Rutherford, CA 94573
Association of growers, producers, negotiants, retailers, and other industry professionals. Reliable source of information on California olive oil.

OLD WAYS PRESERVATION & EXCHANGE TRUST
25 First Street
Cambridge, MA 02141
(617) 621-3000
Education organization that studies traditional diets of various cultures and sponsors research and conferences on various culinary topics. Developed the Mediterranean Diet pyramid.

ORNAMENTAL EDIBLES
3622 Weedin Court
San Jose, CA
Seed catalog, $2.00.

PAPRIKAS WEISS
1572 Second Avenue
New York, NY 10028
(212) 288-6117
Mail-order source for extensive selection of beans, spices, and cheeses.

PARIS-HENRY COUNTY JAYCEES
P. O. Box 444
Paris, TN 38242
Information regarding the World's Biggest Fish Fry.

PEPPER GAL, THE
P. O. Box 23006
Ft. Lauderdale, FL 33307
(305) 537-5540
Scores of pepper seeds, including 120 hot, 60 sweet, and over 30 ornamental seeds.

PETITS PROPOS CULINAIRES
PPC North America
5311 42nd Street, NW
Washington, DC 20015
Culinary periodical.

PINK PEPPERCORN
2686 West Broadway
Vancouver, British Columbia V6K 2G3
(604) 736-4213
Local cookbook store; will special order hard-to-find titles.

POCHE'S MEATMARKET AND
RESTAURANT
Route 2, Box 415
Breaux Bridge, LA 70517
(318) 332-2108
Mail-order source for authentic Cajun meat products, including cracklins, boudin, and churice (chaurice), a hard-to-find sausage.

POWELL'S BOOKS FOR COOKS
3739 Hawthorne Boulevard
Portland, OR 97214
(800) 354-5957
Excellent collection of cookbooks, including some antiques. Newsletter. Mail order.

PROPER MUSTARD, THE
P. O. Box 72
Mount Horeb, WI 53572
(608) 437-3986
Official newsletter of the Mt. Horeb Mustard Museum.

QUE PASA
3315 Cambie Street
Vancouver, British Columbia V5Z 2W6
(604) 874-0064
Retail store specializing in ingredients for Mexican cuisine; cookbooks, too.

RAIN, PATRICIA SPECIALTY FOOD
DISTRIBUTOR
116 Forest Avenue
Santa Cruz, CA 95062
(408) 457-0902
Mail-order source for Tahitian and Bourbon vanilla and vanilla beans; vanilla cookbooks, other vanilla products, too.

ROYAL INTERNATIONAL LTD.
P. O. Box 125
San Juan, TX 78589
(800) 331-7811
Mail-order source for Texas 1015 Supersweet onions. Catalog.

SALT INSTITUTE
Fairfax Plaza, Suite 600
700 North Fairfax
Alexandria, VA 22314-2040
(703) 549-4648
Consumer information on salt.

SEED CORPS, THE
P. O. Box 1705
Santa Rosa, CA 95402
(707) 545-4171
(707) 575-3707 fax
Ian Allison, Director
Solar-start tomato greenhouse.

SEED SAVERS EXCHANGE
3076 North Winn Road
Decorah, IA 52101
Membership, $25.00 U. S., $30.00 Can.
Informational brochure, $1.00.
Genetic preservation program. Members exchange seeds for a small fee; annual yearbook lists all available varieties.

SEEDS BLÜM
Idaho City Stage
Boise, ID 83706
(208) 342-0858
Excellent tomato seeds. Catalog.

SEEDS TRUST/HIGH ALTITUDE GARDENS
P. O. Box 1048
Hailey, ID 83333-1048
Catalog ($3.00) includes Siberian seed stock.

SELECT SONOMA COUNTY
1055 West College Avenue, #194
Santa Rosa, CA 95401
(707) 571-8894
Agricultural marketing organization produces consumers' guidebook to Sonoma County products, including some mail-order sources.

SHEPHERD'S GARDEN SEEDS
30 Irene Street
Torrington, CT 06793
Catalog, $1.00.

SIMPLE COOKING
P. O. Box 88
Steuben, ME 14680-0088
Culinary periodical.

SMITHFIELD COMPANIES, THE
P. O. Box 487
Smithfield, VA 23430
(800) 628-2242
Source for authentic country hams in two styles, Amber Brand Smithfield Ham (smoked and aged for almost a year) and Joyner's Red Eye Country Style Ham (smoked and aged up to three months). Other items, too. Catalog.

SONOMA FOIE GRAS
1905 Sperring Road
Sonoma, CA 95476
(707) 938-1229
Outstanding domestic foie gras, magrait, smoked duck, and other duck products. Mail order. Catalog.

SONOMA PROVENCE EXCHANGE
P.O. Box 1552
Sebastopol, CA 95473
(707) 823-8154
Facilitates cultural, culinary, and agricultural exchange between the sister regions of Sonoma County and Provence.

SOUTH CHINA SEAS TRADING
COMPANY
1689 Johnston Street
Granville Island Market
Box 125
Vancouver, British Columbia V6H 3R9
(604) 681-5402
Specialty retail store carrying supplies for far Eastern cuisine.

SOUTHERN EXPOSURE SEED EXCHANGE
P. O. Box 158
North Garden, VA 22959
(804) 973-4703
Catalog, $3.00.

SPECIALTY FOOD SHOP
555 University Avenue
Toronto, Ontario M5G 1X8
(416) 255-7071
*Specialty foods; cookbooks. Funded by Sick
Childrens Hospital.*

TABASCO COUNTRY STORE
McIlhenny Company
Avery Island, LA 70513
(800) 634-9599
*The first of all Louisiana hot sauce companies
offers a mail-order catalog with the company's
classics as well as an assortment of products not
available elsewhere.*

TANTE MARIE'S COOKING SCHOOL
271 San Francisco Street
San Francisco, CA 94133
(415) 788-6699
*This long-lived cooking school offers both profes-
sional and casual classes 6 days a week.*

TIMBER CREST FARMS
4791 Dry Creek Road
Healdsburg, CA 95448
(707) 433-8251
Ruth Waltenspiel, Owner
*Mail-order dried-tomato products. Wide selection
of other dried foods as well, including cherries,
apricots, pears, nuts, and condiments. Gift baskets, books. Catalog.*

TODARO BROTHERS
555 Second Avenue
New York, NY 10016
(212) 679-7766
Excellent selection of Italian products. Will ship.

TOMATO CLUB, THE
114 East Main Street
Bogota, NJ 07603
(201) 488-2231
(201) 489-4609 fax
*Monthly newsletter for members focuses on grow-
ing tomatoes.*

TOMATO GENETICS RESOURCE
CENTER
Genetic Resources Conservation Program
University of California
Davis, CA 95616
(916) 757-8920
Charles Rick, Curator
*Major international repository for tomato germ
plasm; collection includes over 3,000 varieties,
with about 1,000 from wild stock.*

TOMATO GROWERS SUPPLY COMPANY
P. O. Box 2237
Fort Myers, FL 33902
(813) 768-1119
Catalog, free.

TOOLS & TECHNIQUES
250 16th Street
Vancouver, British Columbia V7V 3R5
(604) 925-1835
(800) 336-2944
*Retail store that carries kitchenware gloriola as
well as specialty foods. They offer cooking classes
and mail order also.*

TOSCANO SONOMA, INC.
1195 Westside Road
Healdsburg, CA 95448
(707) 431-8000
*Producer of California's newest and best extra-
virgin olive oil, DaVero. By appointment only.*

TOTALLY TOMATOES
P. O. Box 1626
Augusta, GA 30903
Everything for the home tomato gardener, including over 300 varieties of seeds (pepper seeds, too), tools, trellises, and strainers. Catalog.

TRAPPEY'S FINE FOODS, INC.
P. O. Box 13610
New Iberia, LA 70562
(800) 365-8727
The makers of Red Devil Louisiana Hot Sauce and a selection of other hot sauces offers a brochure of gift packs and mail order.

UNIVERSITY OF CALIFORNIA AT
BERKELEY WELLNESS LETTER
P. O. Box 420148
Palm Coast, FL 32142
Health-oriented newsletter with reliable information on food.

VIDALIA ONION FESTIVAL
P. O. Box 1213
Vidalia, GA 30474
(912) 537-4466
Information on the festival.

VINEGAR INSTITUTE, THE
64 Perimeter Center East
Atlanta, GA 30346
(404) 393-1340
Consumer information.

VIVANDE PORTA VIA
2125 Filmore Street
San Francisco, CA 94115
(415) 346-4430
Good source for Italian products, including cheeses, olive oils, olives, vinegars, and durum flour. Prepared food and a good café. Catalog.

WILLIAMS-SONOMA
P. O. Box 7456
San Francisco, CA 94120-7456
(800) 541-2233 (for catalog)
Good mail-order source for durum flour, polenta, vanilla beans, high-quality chocolate, culinary equipment, and more. Catalog.

WINE AND FOOD LIBRARY, THE
1207 West Madison
Ann Arbor, MI 48103
(313) 663-4894

WORLD OF COOKBOOKS
1645 South Vineyard Avenue
Los Angeles, CA 90019
Quarterly cookbook-review newsletter.

ZINGERMAN'S DELICATESSEN
422 Detroit Street
Ann Arbor, MI 48104
(313) 663-DELI
Mail-order source for wide variety of products, including English mustards and Italian imports. Catalog.

The Good Cook's

Archives

memorable meals

DATE _____ OCCASION _____

LOCATION _____

COMPANIONS _____

_____

MENU _____

_____

_____

_____

COMMENTS _____

_____

_____

_____

_____

DATE _____ OCCASION _____

LOCATION _____

COMPANIONS _____

_____

MENU _____

_____

_____

_____

COMMENTS _____

_____

_____

_____

DATE _____ OCCASION _____

LOCATION _____

COMPANIONS _____

_____

MENU _____

_____

_____

_____

COMMENTS _____

_____

_____

_____

_____

_____

DATE _____ OCCASION _____

LOCATION _____

COMPANIONS _____

_____

MENU _____

_____

_____

_____

COMMENTS _____

_____

_____

_____

_____

Only dull people are brilliant at breakfast.
—OSCAR WILDE

DATE _____ OCCASION _____

LOCATION _____

COMPANIONS _____

_____

MENU _____

_____

_____

_____

COMMENTS _____

_____

_____

_____

_____

DATE _____ OCCASION _____

LOCATION _____

COMPANIONS _____

_____

MENU _____

_____

_____

_____

COMMENTS _____

_____

_____

_____

_____

DATE _____ OCCASION _____

LOCATION _____

COMPANIONS _____

_____

MENU _____

_____

_____

_____

COMMENTS _____

_____

_____

_____

_____

_____

DATE _____ OCCASION _____

LOCATION _____

COMPANIONS _____

_____

MENU _____

_____

_____

_____

COMMENTS _____

_____

_____

_____

_____

_____

DATE _____ OCCASION _____

LOCATION _____

COMPANIONS _____

_____

MENU _____

_____

_____

_____

COMMENTS _____

_____

_____

_____

_____

_____

DATE _____ OCCASION _____

LOCATION _____

COMPANIONS _____

_____

MENU _____

_____

_____

_____

COMMENTS _____

_____

_____

_____

_____

_____

DATE _____ OCCASION _____

LOCATION _____

COMPANIONS _____

_____

MENU _____

_____

_____

_____

_____

COMMENTS _____

_____

_____

_____

_____

The Mediterranean Diet has enjoyed tremendous press in recent years, and well it should. Not only is there substantial evidence of the health benefits of this style of eating, but it is also easy to maintain and thoroughly delightful. Keep its basic structure in mind as you plan your menus: use olive oil as your primary fat; include an abundance of complex carbohydrates like breads, grains, beans, and pasta; serve a salad at every meal; use a wide variety of vegetables; serve meat only occasionally, but serve cheese and yogurt regularly; enjoy wine as a regular part of meals; and don't forget to exercise. Omit or drastically decrease your use of butter and cream and entirely eliminate milk, except for a bit in your tea or coffee.

DATE _____ OCCASION _____

LOCATION _____

COMPANIONS _____

_____

MENU _____

_____

_____

_____

COMMENTS _____

_____

_____

_____

_____

DATE _____ OCCASION _____

LOCATION _____

COMPANIONS _____

_____

MENU _____

_____

_____

_____

COMMENTS _____

_____

_____

_____

_____

DATE _____ OCCASION _____

LOCATION _____

COMPANIONS _____

_____

MENU _____

_____

_____

_____

COMMENTS _____

_____

_____

_____

_____

DATE _____ OCCASION _____

LOCATION _____

COMPANIONS _____

_____

MENU _____

_____

_____

_____

COMMENTS _____

_____

_____

_____

_____

DATE _____ OCCASION _____

LOCATION _____

COMPANIONS _____

_____

MENU _____

_____

_____

_____

COMMENTS _____

_____

_____

_____

_____

DATE _____ OCCASION _____

LOCATION _____

COMPANIONS _____

_____

MENU _____

_____

_____

_____

COMMENTS _____

_____

_____

_____

_____

DATE _____ OCCASION _____

LOCATION _____

COMPANIONS _____

_____

MENU _____

_____

_____

_____

COMMENTS _____

_____

_____

_____

_____

*I feel now that gastronomical perfection can be reached
in these combinations: one person dining alone, usually
upon a couch or a hill side; two people, of no matter
what sex or age, dining in a good restaurant; six people,
of no matter what sex or age, dining in a good home.*
—*M. F. K. FISHER*, An Alphabet for Gourmets

favorite foods &
important dates

NAME _____ BIRTHDAY/ANNIVERSARY _____

FAVORITE FOODS/RESTAURANTS _____

_____

FAVORITE BEVERAGES _____

FOOD PHOBIAS _____

_____

NAME _____ BIRTHDAY/ANNIVERSARY _____

FAVORITE FOODS/RESTAURANTS _____

_____

FAVORITE BEVERAGES _____

FOOD PHOBIAS _____

_____

NAME _____ BIRTHDAY/ANNIVERSARY _____

FAVORITE FOODS/RESTAURANTS _____

_____

FAVORITE BEVERAGES _____

FOOD PHOBIAS _____

_____

Somehow I have never minded dining alone. Instead, I find it is a rare opportunity for relaxing and collecting my senses, and I have always made each occasion something of a ceremony. A nicely set table and time—these are as important as the food.

—JAMES BEARD, Delights and Prejudices

NAME _____ BIRTHDAY/ANNIVERSARY _____
FAVORITE FOODS/RESTAURANTS _____
_____
FAVORITE BEVERAGES _____
FOOD PHOBIAS _____
_____

NAME _____ BIRTHDAY/ANNIVERSARY _____
FAVORITE FOODS/RESTAURANTS _____
_____
FAVORITE BEVERAGES _____
FOOD PHOBIAS _____
_____

NAME _____ BIRTHDAY/ANNIVERSARY _____
FAVORITE FOODS/RESTAURANTS _____
_____
FAVORITE BEVERAGES _____
FOOD PHOBIAS _____
_____

NAME _____ BIRTHDAY/ANNIVERSARY _____

FAVORITE FOODS/RESTAURANTS _____

_____

FAVORITE BEVERAGES _____

FOOD PHOBIAS _____

_____

NAME _____ BIRTHDAY/ANNIVERSARY _____

FAVORITE FOODS/RESTAURANTS _____

_____

FAVORITE BEVERAGES _____

FOOD PHOBIAS _____

_____

NAME _____ BIRTHDAY/ANNIVERSARY _____

FAVORITE FOODS/RESTAURANTS _____

_____

FAVORITE BEVERAGES _____

FOOD PHOBIAS _____

_____

NAME _____ BIRTHDAY/ANNIVERSARY _____

FAVORITE FOODS/RESTAURANTS _____

_____

FAVORITE BEVERAGES _____

FOOD PHOBIAS _____

_____

NAME _____ BIRTHDAY/ANNIVERSARY _____
FAVORITE FOODS/RESTAURANTS _____
_____
FAVORITE BEVERAGES _____
FOOD PHOBIAS _____
_____

NAME _____ BIRTHDAY/ANNIVERSARY _____
FAVORITE FOODS/RESTAURANTS _____
_____
FAVORITE BEVERAGES _____
FOOD PHOBIAS _____
_____

NAME _____ BIRTHDAY/ANNIVERSARY _____
FAVORITE FOODS/RESTAURANTS _____
_____
FAVORITE BEVERAGES _____
FOOD PHOBIAS _____
_____

NAME _____ BIRTHDAY/ANNIVERSARY _____
FAVORITE FOODS/RESTAURANTS _____
_____
FAVORITE BEVERAGES _____
FOOD PHOBIAS _____
_____

NAME _____ BIRTHDAY/ANNIVERSARY _____

FAVORITE FOODS/RESTAURANTS _____

_____

FAVORITE BEVERAGES _____

FOOD PHOBIAS _____

_____

NAME _____ BIRTHDAY/ANNIVERSARY _____

FAVORITE FOODS/RESTAURANTS _____

_____

FAVORITE BEVERAGES _____

FOOD PHOBIAS _____

_____

NAME _____ BIRTHDAY/ANNIVERSARY _____

FAVORITE FOODS/RESTAURANTS _____

_____

FAVORITE BEVERAGES _____

FOOD PHOBIAS _____

_____

Dinner: A major daily activity, which can be accomplished in worthy fashion only by intelligent people. It is not enough to eat. To dine, there must be diversified, calm conversation. It should sparkle with the rubies of the wine between courses, be deliciously suave with the sweetness of dessert, and acquire true profundity with the coffee.

—Alexander Dumas's Dictionary of Cuisine

entertaining

OCCASION _____

DATE _____

TIME _____

GUESTS

_____

_____

_____

_____

_____

MENU

_____

_____

_____

_____

_____

_____

WINES/BEVERAGES

_____

_____

_____

_____

NOTES _____

_____

_____

_____

_____

OCCASION _____

DATE _____

TIME _____

GUESTS

_____

_____

_____

_____

_____

MENU

_____

_____

_____

_____

_____

WINES/BEVERAGES

_____

_____

_____

_____

NOTES _____

_____

_____

_____

_____

OCCASION _____

DATE _____

TIME _____

GUESTS

_____

_____

_____

_____

_____

MENU

_____

_____

_____

_____

_____

WINES/BEVERAGES

_____

_____

_____

_____

NOTES _____

_____

_____

_____

_____

*Noncooks think it's silly to invest two
hours' work in two minutes' enjoyment;
but if cooking is evanescent, well, so is
the ballet.*
—JULIA CHILD

OCCASION _____

DATE _____

TIME _____

GUESTS

_____
_____
_____
_____
_____

MENU

_____
_____
_____
_____
_____

WINES/BEVERAGES

_____
_____
_____
_____

NOTES _____
_____
_____
_____

OCCASION _____

DATE _____

TIME _____

GUESTS

_____

_____

_____

_____

_____

MENU

_____

_____

_____

_____

_____

_____

WINES/BEVERAGES

_____

_____

_____

_____

NOTES _____

_____

_____

_____

_____

OCCASION _____

DATE _____

TIME _____

GUESTS

_____

_____

_____

_____

_____

_____

MENU

_____

_____

_____

_____

_____

_____

WINES/BEVERAGES

_____

_____

_____

_____

NOTES _____

_____

_____

_____

_____

OCCASION _____

DATE _____

TIME _____

GUESTS

_____

_____

_____

_____

_____

MENU

_____

_____

_____

_____

_____

_____

WINES/BEVERAGES

_____

_____

_____

_____

NOTES _____

_____

_____

_____

_____

OCCASION _____

DATE _____

TIME _____

GUESTS

_____

_____

_____

_____

_____

MENU

_____

_____

_____

_____

_____

_____

WINES/BEVERAGES

_____

_____

_____

_____

NOTES _____

_____

_____

_____

_____

Instead of butter, serve extra-virgin olive oil as a condiment with bread, which should be of the dense, chewy, crusty variety. Add a bit of kosher salt and freshly ground black pepper to the oil and, for variety, a splash of balsamic vinegar. It is much better than butter, and healthier, too.

OCCASION _____

DATE _____

TIME _____

GUESTS

_____

_____

_____

_____

_____

MENU

_____

_____

_____

_____

_____

WINES/BEVERAGES

_____

_____

_____

NOTES _____

_____

_____

_____

_____

OCCASION _____

DATE _____

TIME _____

GUESTS

_____

_____

_____

_____

_____

MENU

_____

_____

_____

_____

_____

_____

WINES/BEVERAGES

_____

_____

_____

_____

NOTES _____

_____

_____

_____

_____

OCCASION _____

DATE _____

TIME _____

GUESTS

_____

_____

_____

_____

_____

MENU

_____

_____

_____

_____

_____

_____

WINES/BEVERAGES

_____

_____

_____

_____

NOTES _____

_____

_____

_____

_____

OCCASION _____

DATE _____

TIME _____

GUESTS

_____

_____

_____

_____

_____

MENU

_____

_____

_____

_____

_____

WINES/BEVERAGES

_____

_____

_____

_____

NOTES _____

_____

_____

_____

_____

Good manners, like good taste, derive from sensibility and simple common sense. Once mastered, that concept can be abiding and guiding. For example, it is polite to answer invitations promptly, not to wait to see if something more to your liking comes up. Similarly, it is polite to arrive on time.
—CRAIG CLAIBORNE, Elements of Etiquette

OCCASION _____

DATE _____

TIME _____

GUESTS

_____

_____

_____

_____

_____

MENU

_____

_____

_____

_____

_____

_____

WINES/BEVERAGES

_____

_____

_____

_____

NOTES _____

_____

_____

_____

_____

the pleasures of summer

lavender

shade

tomatoes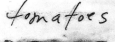

gardens

watermelon

a cat or a sunbeam

bowl of olives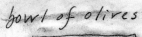

fountain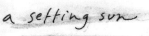

a cool place to eat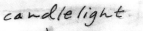

wine

a setting sun

candlelight

favorite spring recipes

ASPARAGUS • STRAWBERRIES • SNOW PEAS • BABY LEEKS •

SPRING LAMB • WILD MUSTARD GREENS • MORELS

RECIPE NAME	SOURCE BOOK/MAGAZINE	PAGE

favorite summer recipes

BERRIES • MELONS • WILD SALMON • TOMATOES • APRICOTS •

NECTARINES • PEACHES • FRESH TUNA • GARLIC • PEPPERS

RECIPE NAME	SOURCE BOOK/MAGAZINE	PAGE

favorite fall recipes

POMEGRANATES • CRANBERRIES • PUMPKINS •

NEW OLIVE OIL • FIGS

RECIPE NAME	SOURCE BOOK/MAGAZINE	PAGE

favorite winter recipes

PERSIMMONS • FRESH TRUFFLES • OYSTERS • CRAB •

ROOT VEGETABLES • BLOOD ORANGES

RECIPE NAME	SOURCE BOOK/MAGAZINE	PAGE

favorite poultry recipes

ROASTED CHICKEN • TEA-SMOKED DUCK • TURKEY GUMBO •

GRILLED QUAIL • BRAISED CAPON

RECIPE NAME	SOURCE BOOK/MAGAZINE	PAGE

favorite meat recipes

STEAK TARTARE • BARBECUED RIBS • BRAISED LAMB SHANKS •

STUFFED PORK LOIN • VENISON STEW

RECIPE NAME	SOURCE BOOK/MAGAZINE	PAGE

favorite sauce recipes

Vinaigrette • Marinade • Mayonnaise • Salsa •

Tomato Sauce • Gravy • Cream Sauce • Caramel Sauce

RECIPE NAME	SOURCE BOOK/MAGAZINE	PAGE

favorite dessert recipes

Bread Pudding • Lemon Ice • Chocolate Mousse • Pecan Pie • Raspberry Strudel • Crème Brûlée

RECIPE NAME	SOURCE BOOK/MAGAZINE	PAGE

cookbooks on loan

GENERAL • SINGLE SUBJECT • BAKING • ETHNIC •

TECHNICAL • SCIENTIFIC • LITERARY

AUTHOR   TITLE   PUBLISHER

SUBJECT/NOTES_____

_____

_____

BORROWED BY _____ PHONE NUMBER _____

AUTHOR   TITLE   PUBLISHER

SUBJECT/NOTES_____

_____

_____

BORROWED BY _____ PHONE NUMBER _____

AUTHOR   TITLE   PUBLISHER

SUBJECT/NOTES_____

_____

_____

BORROWED BY _____ PHONE NUMBER _____

AUTHOR TITLE PUBLISHER

SUBJECT/NOTES _____

_____

_____

BORROWED BY _____ PHONE NUMBER _____

AUTHOR TITLE PUBLISHER

SUBJECT/NOTES _____

_____

_____

BORROWED BY _____ PHONE NUMBER _____

AUTHOR TITLE PUBLISHER

SUBJECT/NOTES _____

_____

_____

BORROWED BY _____ PHONE NUMBER _____

AUTHOR TITLE PUBLISHER

SUBJECT/NOTES _____

_____

_____

BORROWED BY _____ PHONE NUMBER _____

Next to eating good dinners, a healthy man with a benevolent turn of mind, must like, I think, to read about them.

—WILLIAM MAKEPEACE THACKERAY

AUTHOR   TITLE   PUBLISHER

SUBJECT/NOTES

BORROWED BY   PHONE NUMBER

AUTHOR   TITLE   PUBLISHER

SUBJECT/NOTES

BORROWED BY   PHONE NUMBER

AUTHOR   TITLE   PUBLISHER

SUBJECT/NOTES

BORROWED BY   PHONE NUMBER

AUTHOR   TITLE   PUBLISHER
SUBJECT/NOTES_____

_____

_____

BORROWED BY _____ PHONE NUMBER _____

AUTHOR   TITLE   PUBLISHER
SUBJECT/NOTES_____

_____

_____

BORROWED BY _____ PHONE NUMBER _____

AUTHOR   TITLE   PUBLISHER
SUBJECT/NOTES_____

_____

_____

BORROWED BY _____ PHONE NUMBER _____

AUTHOR   TITLE   PUBLISHER
SUBJECT/NOTES_____

_____

_____

BORROWED BY _____ PHONE NUMBER _____

AUTHOR   TITLE   PUBLISHER

SUBJECT/NOTES_____

_____

_____

BORROWED BY _____ PHONE NUMBER _____

AUTHOR   TITLE   PUBLISHER

SUBJECT/NOTES_____

_____

_____

BORROWED BY _____ PHONE NUMBER _____

AUTHOR   TITLE   PUBLISHER

SUBJECT/NOTES_____

_____

_____

BORROWED BY _____ PHONE NUMBER _____

AUTHOR   TITLE   PUBLISHER

SUBJECT/NOTES_____

_____

_____

BORROWED BY _____ PHONE NUMBER _____

AUTHOR   TITLE   PUBLISHER

SUBJECT/NOTES_____

_____

_____

BORROWED BY _____ PHONE NUMBER _____

AUTHOR   TITLE   PUBLISHER

SUBJECT/NOTES_____

_____

_____

BORROWED BY _____ PHONE NUMBER _____

AUTHOR   TITLE   PUBLISHER

SUBJECT/NOTES_____

_____

_____

BORROWED BY _____ PHONE NUMBER _____

No restaurants. The means of consoling oneself: reading cookbooks.

—Charles Baudelaire

The Good Cook's
Wine Cellar

There is no money, among that which I have spent since I began to earn my living, of the expenditure of which I am less ashamed, or which gave me better value in return, than the price of the liquids chronicled in this booklet. When they were good they pleased my senses, cheered my spirits, improved my moral and intellectual powers, besides enabling me to confer the same benefit on other people.

—GEORGE SAINTSBURY, Notes on a Cellar-Book

NAME OF WINE _____ PURCHASED AT _____

VINTNER _____ VINTAGE _____

COUNTRY/STATE/COUNTY OF ORIGIN _____

VARIETAL _____ # OF BOTTLES PURCHASED _____

DATE OPENED _____ SHARED WITH _____

TASTING NOTES _____

_____

NAME OF WINE _____ PURCHASED AT _____

VINTNER _____ VINTAGE _____

COUNTRY/STATE/COUNTY OF ORIGIN _____

VARIETAL _____ # OF BOTTLES PURCHASED _____

DATE OPENED _____ SHARED WITH _____

TASTING NOTES _____

_____

NAME OF WINE _____ PURCHASED AT _____

VINTNER _____ VINTAGE _____

COUNTRY/STATE/COUNTY OF ORIGIN _____

VARIETAL _____ # OF BOTTLES PURCHASED _____

DATE OPENED _____ SHARED WITH _____

TASTING NOTES _____

No nation is drunken where wine is cheap; and none sober, where the dearness of wine substitutes ardent spirits as the common beverage. It is, in truth, the only antidote to the bane of whiskey.
—THOMAS JEFFERSON

NAME OF WINE _____ PURCHASED AT _____

VINTNER _____ VINTAGE _____

COUNTRY/STATE/COUNTY OF ORIGIN _____

VARIETAL _____ # OF BOTTLES PURCHASED _____

DATE OPENED _____ SHARED WITH _____

TASTING NOTES _____

_____

Store wine in a cool place away from light and where the temperature remains fairly constant. Frequent, wide fluctuations in temperature can damage a wine fairly quickly. Of course, a wine cellar is ideal, but how many of us have cellars these days? If you're serious about wine, consult a reliable publication or a local wine merchant about the best ways to store wine for a long period.

NAME OF WINE _____ PURCHASED AT _____

VINTNER _____ VINTAGE _____

COUNTRY/STATE/COUNTY OF ORIGIN _____

VARIETAL _____ # OF BOTTLES PURCHASED _____

DATE OPENED _____ SHARED WITH _____

TASTING NOTES _____

_____

NAME OF WINE _____ PURCHASED AT _____

VINTNER _____ VINTAGE _____

COUNTRY/STATE/COUNTY OF ORIGIN _____

VARIETAL _____ # OF BOTTLES PURCHASED _____

DATE OPENED _____ SHARED WITH _____

TASTING NOTES _____

_____

NAME OF WINE _____ PURCHASED AT _____

VINTNER _____ VINTAGE _____

COUNTRY/STATE/COUNTY OF ORIGIN _____

VARIETAL _____ # OF BOTTLES PURCHASED _____

DATE OPENED _____ SHARED WITH _____

TASTING NOTES _____

_____

NAME OF WINE _____ PURCHASED AT _____

VINTNER _____ VINTAGE _____

COUNTRY/STATE/COUNTY OF ORIGIN _____

VARIETAL _____ # OF BOTTLES PURCHASED _____

DATE OPENED _____ SHARED WITH _____

TASTING NOTES _____

_____

NAME OF WINE _____ PURCHASED AT _____

VINTNER _____ VINTAGE _____

COUNTRY/STATE/COUNTY OF ORIGIN _____

VARIETAL _____ # OF BOTTLES PURCHASED _____

DATE OPENED _____ SHARED WITH _____

TASTING NOTES _____

_____

NAME OF WINE _____ PURCHASED AT _____

VINTNER _____ VINTAGE _____

COUNTRY/STATE/COUNTY OF ORIGIN _____

VARIETAL _____ # OF BOTTLES PURCHASED _____

DATE OPENED _____ SHARED WITH _____

TASTING NOTES _____

_____

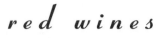

NAME OF WINE _____ PURCHASED AT _____

VINTNER _____ VINTAGE _____

COUNTRY/STATE/COUNTY OF ORIGIN _____

VARIETAL _____ # OF BOTTLES PURCHASED _____

DATE OPENED _____ SHARED WITH _____

TASTING NOTES _____

_____

NAME OF WINE _____ PURCHASED AT _____

VINTNER _____ VINTAGE _____

COUNTRY/STATE/COUNTY OF ORIGIN _____

VARIETAL _____ # OF BOTTLES PURCHASED _____

DATE OPENED _____ SHARED WITH _____

TASTING NOTES _____

_____

NAME OF WINE _____ PURCHASED AT _____

VINTNER _____ VINTAGE _____

COUNTRY/STATE/COUNTY OF ORIGIN _____

VARIETAL _____ # OF BOTTLES PURCHASED _____

DATE OPENED _____ SHARED WITH _____

TASTING NOTES _____

_____

Friends don't let friends drink chardonnay.
—RANDALL GRAHAM, BONNY DOON VINEYARDS

NAME OF WINE _____ PURCHASED AT _____

VINTNER _____ VINTAGE _____

COUNTRY/STATE/COUNTY OF ORIGIN _____

VARIETAL _____ # OF BOTTLES PURCHASED _____

DATE OPENED _____ SHARED WITH _____

TASTING NOTES _____

_____

> *In Europe we thought of wine as something as healthy and normal as food and also as a great giver of happiness and well being and delight. Drinking wine was not a snobbism nor a sign of sophistication nor a cult; it was as natural as eating and to me as necessary.*
>
> —ERNEST HEMINGWAY, A Moveable Feast

NAME OF WINE _____ PURCHASED AT _____

VINTNER _____ VINTAGE _____

COUNTRY/STATE/COUNTY OF ORIGIN _____

VARIETAL _____ # OF BOTTLES PURCHASED _____

DATE OPENED _____ SHARED WITH _____

TASTING NOTES _____

_____

NAME OF WINE _____ PURCHASED AT _____

VINTNER _____ VINTAGE _____

COUNTRY/STATE/COUNTY OF ORIGIN _____

VARIETAL _____ # OF BOTTLES PURCHASED _____

DATE OPENED _____ SHARED WITH _____

TASTING NOTES _____

_____

NAME OF WINE _____ PURCHASED AT _____

VINTNER _____ VINTAGE _____

COUNTRY/STATE/COUNTY OF ORIGIN _____

VARIETAL _____ # OF BOTTLES PURCHASED _____

DATE OPENED _____ SHARED WITH _____

TASTING NOTES _____

_____

NAME OF WINE _____ PURCHASED AT _____

VINTNER _____ VINTAGE _____

COUNTRY/STATE/COUNTY OF ORIGIN _____

VARIETAL _____ # OF BOTTLES PURCHASED _____

DATE OPENED _____ SHARED WITH _____

TASTING NOTES _____

_____

*One should always be drunk. That's the great thing;
the only question. Not to feel the horrible burden of
Time weighing on your shoulders and bowing you to
the earth, you should be drunk without respite. Drunk with
what? With wine, with poetry, or with virtue, as you please.
But get drunk.*

—CHARLES BAUDELAIRE, "GET DRUNK"

NAME OF WINE _____ PURCHASED AT _____

VINTNER _____ VINTAGE _____

COUNTRY/STATE/COUNTY OF ORIGIN _____

VARIETAL _____ # OF BOTTLES PURCHASED _____

DATE OPENED _____ SHARED WITH _____

TASTING NOTES _____

_____

NAME OF WINE _____ PURCHASED AT _____

VINTNER _____ VINTAGE _____

COUNTRY/STATE/COUNTY OF ORIGIN _____

VARIETAL _____ # OF BOTTLES PURCHASED _____

DATE OPENED _____ SHARED WITH _____

TASTING NOTES _____

_____

NAME OF WINE _____ PURCHASED AT _____

VINTNER _____ VINTAGE _____

COUNTRY/STATE/COUNTY OF ORIGIN _____

VARIETAL _____ # OF BOTTLES PURCHASED _____

DATE OPENED _____ SHARED WITH _____

TASTING NOTES _____

_____

NAME OF WINE _____ PURCHASED AT _____

VINTNER _____ VINTAGE _____

COUNTRY/STATE/COUNTY OF ORIGIN _____

VARIETAL _____ # OF BOTTLES PURCHASED _____

DATE OPENED _____ SHARED WITH _____

TASTING NOTES _____

_____

NAME OF WINE _____ PURCHASED AT _____

VINTNER _____ VINTAGE _____

COUNTRY/STATE/COUNTY OF ORIGIN _____

VARIETAL _____ # OF BOTTLES PURCHASED _____

DATE OPENED _____ SHARED WITH _____

TASTING NOTES _____

_____

NAME OF WINE _____ PURCHASED AT _____

VINTNER _____ VINTAGE _____

COUNTRY/STATE/COUNTY OF ORIGIN _____

VARIETAL _____ # OF BOTTLES PURCHASED _____

DATE OPENED _____ SHARED WITH _____

TASTING NOTES _____

_____

Abstainers and heavy drinkers die sooner of all causes and are hit with crippling or lethal heart attacks at almost twice the rate as their moderately sipping neighbors.

—Lewis Perdue, The French Paradox and Beyond

NAME OF WINE _____ PURCHASED AT _____

VINTNER _____ VINTAGE _____

COUNTRY/STATE/COUNTY OF ORIGIN _____

VARIETAL _____ # OF BOTTLES PURCHASED _____

DATE OPENED _____ SHARED WITH _____

TASTING NOTES _____

_____

NAME OF WINE _____ PURCHASED AT _____

VINTNER _____ VINTAGE _____

COUNTRY/STATE/COUNTY OF ORIGIN _____

VARIETAL _____ # OF BOTTLES PURCHASED _____

DATE OPENED _____ SHARED WITH _____

TASTING NOTES _____

_____

NAME OF WINE _____ PURCHASED AT _____

VINTNER _____ VINTAGE _____

COUNTRY/STATE/COUNTY OF ORIGIN _____

VARIETAL _____ # OF BOTTLES PURCHASED _____

DATE OPENED _____ SHARED WITH _____

TASTING NOTES _____

_____

NAME OF WINE _____ PURCHASED AT _____

VINTNER _____ VINTAGE _____

COUNTRY/STATE/COUNTY OF ORIGIN _____

VARIETAL _____ # OF BOTTLES PURCHASED _____

DATE OPENED _____ SHARED WITH _____

TASTING NOTES _____

_____

NAME OF WINE _____ PURCHASED AT _____

VINTNER _____ VINTAGE _____

COUNTRY/STATE/COUNTY OF ORIGIN _____

VARIETAL _____ # OF BOTTLES PURCHASED _____

DATE OPENED _____ SHARED WITH _____

TASTING NOTES _____

_____

> *At their best, pinot noirs are the most romantic of wines, with so voluptuous a perfume, so sweet an edge, and so powerful a punch that, like falling in love, they make the blood run hot and the soul wax embarrassingly poetic.*
>
> —*JOEL FLEISHMAN*, Vanity Fair, *August 1991*

NAME OF WINE _____ PURCHASED AT _____

VINTNER _____ VINTAGE _____

COUNTRY/STATE/COUNTY OF ORIGIN _____

VARIETAL _____ # OF BOTTLES PURCHASED _____

DATE OPENED _____ SHARED WITH _____

TASTING NOTES _____

_____

Knowing a wine's vintage [the year the wine was made] can tell you much about the kind of wine. But menu-planners make the common mistake of paying attention only to the quality ratings that vintages receive on vintage charts; they assume that only top-rated vintages are suitable for drinking with food. Nothing could be further from the truth. Very often, a wine from a lesser vintage . . . will behave itself better at table than a wine from a top-rated vintage. . . . You can save a lot of money—and elicit a lot of pleasure and surprise—by serving off-vintage wines with your meals.

—DAVID ROSENGARTEN AND JOSHUA WESSON, Red Wine with Fish

NAME OF WINE _____ PURCHASED AT _____

VINTNER _____ VINTAGE _____

COUNTRY/STATE/COUNTY OF ORIGIN _____

VARIETAL _____ # OF BOTTLES PURCHASED _____

DATE OPENED _____ SHARED WITH _____

TASTING NOTES _____

_____

NAME OF WINE _____ PURCHASED AT _____

VINTNER _____ VINTAGE _____

COUNTRY/STATE/COUNTY OF ORIGIN _____

VARIETAL _____ # OF BOTTLES PURCHASED _____

DATE OPENED _____ SHARED WITH _____

TASTING NOTES _____

_____

NAME OF WINE _____ PURCHASED AT _____

VINTNER _____ VINTAGE _____

COUNTRY/STATE/COUNTY OF ORIGIN _____

VARIETAL _____ # OF BOTTLES PURCHASED _____

DATE OPENED _____ SHARED WITH _____

TASTING NOTES _____

_____

NAME OF WINE _____ PURCHASED AT _____

VINTNER _____ VINTAGE _____

COUNTRY/STATE/COUNTY OF ORIGIN _____

VARIETAL _____ # OF BOTTLES PURCHASED _____

DATE OPENED _____ SHARED WITH _____

TASTING NOTES _____

_____

NAME OF WINE _____ PURCHASED AT _____

VINTNER _____ VINTAGE _____

COUNTRY/STATE/COUNTY OF ORIGIN _____

VARIETAL _____ # OF BOTTLES PURCHASED _____

DATE OPENED _____ SHARED WITH _____

TASTING NOTES _____

_____

Pinot noir is the James Dean of wine; it's the wine women who love too much can't drink. Pinot noir is Oscar Wilde, David Janssen, Marlene Dietrich, all in your living room at the same time. Pinot noir is Cathy and Heathcliff; it's Juliet on her wedding night. It's Connie Chatterley in the rain, wearing nothing but a pair of red shoes. In its finest vintages, pinot noir is Lord Peter with Harriet in a wine-red frock.

—MICHELE ANNA JORDAN, "SEX AND A SINGLE GRAPE"

sparkling wines

NAME OF WINE _____ PURCHASED AT _____

VINTNER _____ VINTAGE _____

COUNTRY/STATE/COUNTY OF ORIGIN _____

VARIETAL _____ # OF BOTTLES PURCHASED _____

DATE OPENED _____ SHARED WITH _____

TASTING NOTES _____

_____

NAME OF WINE _____ PURCHASED AT _____

VINTNER _____ VINTAGE _____

COUNTRY/STATE/COUNTY OF ORIGIN _____

VARIETAL _____ # OF BOTTLES PURCHASED _____

DATE OPENED _____ SHARED WITH _____

TASTING NOTES _____

_____

NAME OF WINE _____ PURCHASED AT _____

VINTNER _____ VINTAGE _____

COUNTRY/STATE/COUNTY OF ORIGIN _____

VARIETAL _____ # OF BOTTLES PURCHASED _____

DATE OPENED _____ SHARED WITH _____

TASTING NOTES _____

_____

In a pinch, you can always use a wine bottle as a rolling pin.
—*LAURIE COLWIN,* Home Cooking

Champagne *refers to a specific wine-growing region in northern France, where* méthode champenoise, *the technique for producing the finest-quality sparkling wines, was developed. The bubbles in this wine are produced by carbon dioxide trapped inside a tightly corked bottle in a process that is both labor-intensive and time-consuming, hence the quality and the price of wines produced by this technique. There are quicker methods of producing sparkling wines, but they all lack the elegance and the finesse of true* méthode champenoise *sparkling wines.*

NAME OF WINE _____ PURCHASED AT _____

VINTNER _____ VINTAGE _____

COUNTRY/STATE/COUNTY OF ORIGIN _____

VARIETAL _____ # OF BOTTLES PURCHASED _____

DATE OPENED _____ SHARED WITH _____

TASTING NOTES _____

_____

NAME OF WINE _____ PURCHASED AT _____

VINTNER _____ VINTAGE _____

COUNTRY/STATE/COUNTY OF ORIGIN _____

VARIETAL _____ # OF BOTTLES PURCHASED _____

DATE OPENED _____ SHARED WITH _____

TASTING NOTES _____

_____

NAME OF WINE _____ PURCHASED AT _____

VINTNER _____ VINTAGE _____

COUNTRY/STATE/COUNTY OF ORIGIN _____

VARIETAL _____ # OF BOTTLES PURCHASED _____

DATE OPENED _____ SHARED WITH _____

TASTING NOTES _____

dessert wines

NAME OF WINE _____ PURCHASED AT _____

VINTNER _____ VINTAGE _____

COUNTRY/STATE/COUNTY OF ORIGIN _____

VARIETAL _____ # OF BOTTLES PURCHASED _____

DATE OPENED _____ SHARED WITH _____

TASTING NOTES _____

_____

NAME OF WINE _____ PURCHASED AT _____

VINTNER _____ VINTAGE _____

COUNTRY/STATE/COUNTY OF ORIGIN _____

VARIETAL _____ # OF BOTTLES PURCHASED _____

DATE OPENED _____ SHARED WITH _____

TASTING NOTES _____

_____

NAME OF WINE _____ PURCHASED AT _____

VINTNER _____ VINTAGE _____

COUNTRY/STATE/COUNTY OF ORIGIN _____

VARIETAL _____ # OF BOTTLES PURCHASED _____

DATE OPENED _____ SHARED WITH _____

TASTING NOTES _____

_____

 In relation to wine, the term dry *simply means not sweet, an important consideration when pairing wine and food.*

There are some fairly safe generalizations that can be made about wine. So far as we know, it was the first alcoholic beverage known to man. The process of making it is relatively simple. It is the indispensable accompaniment to good food. He who challenges the first two will be duly credited with superior knowledge; but anyone who attempts to confute the third is just simply a fool.

—ANGELO PELLEGRINI, The Unprejudiced Palate

NAME OF WINE _____ PURCHASED AT _____

VINTNER _____ VINTAGE _____

COUNTRY/STATE/COUNTY OF ORIGIN _____

VARIETAL _____ # OF BOTTLES PURCHASED _____

DATE OPENED _____ SHARED WITH _____

TASTING NOTES _____

_____

NAME OF WINE _____ PURCHASED AT _____

VINTNER _____ VINTAGE _____

COUNTRY/STATE/COUNTY OF ORIGIN _____

VARIETAL _____ # OF BOTTLES PURCHASED _____

DATE OPENED _____ SHARED WITH _____

TASTING NOTES _____

_____

NAME OF WINE _____ PURCHASED AT _____

VINTNER _____ VINTAGE _____

COUNTRY/STATE/COUNTY OF ORIGIN _____

VARIETAL _____ # OF BOTTLES PURCHASED _____

DATE OPENED _____ SHARED WITH _____

TASTING NOTES _____

_____